ANGRY
LIKE JONAH

Books by Corrine Vanderwerff

Way to Go!
Kill Thy Neighbor (Pacific Press)
Angry Like Jonah

To order, call 1-800-765-6955.

Visit us at www.rhpa.org for more information on
Review and Herald products.

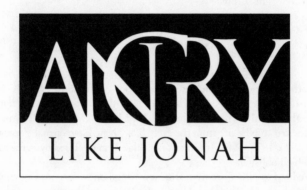

ANGRY
LIKE JONAH

FINDING HEALING FOR

ANGRY FEELINGS

CORRINE VANDERWERFF

REVIEW AND HERALD® PUBLISHING ASSOCIATION
HAGERSTOWN, MD 21740

Unless otherwise noted, Bible texts in this book are from the New Revised
Standard Version of the Bible, copyright © 1989 by the Division of Christian Education
of the National Council of the Churches of Christ in the U.S.A. Used by permission.
Texts credited to NIV are from the *Holy Bible, New International Version*.
Copyright © 1973, 1978, 1984, International Bible Society. Used by permission of
Zondervan Bible Publishers.
Texts credited to NKJV are from the New King James Version. Copyright © 1979,
1980, 1982 by Thomas Nelson, Inc. Used by permission. All rights reserved.
Bible texts credited to TEV are from the *Good News Bible*—Old Testament:
Copyright © American Bible Society 1976; New Testament: Copyright © American
Bible Society 1966, 1971, 1976.

This book was
Edited by Gerald Wheeler
Copyedited by William Cleveland and James Cavil
Designed by Willie Duke
Cover photo by Alan Thornton/Tony Stone Images
Typeset: 12/15 Goudy

PRINTED IN U.S.A.

02 01 00 99 98   5 4 3 2 1

R&H Cataloging Service
Vanderwerff, Corrine Belle (Kandoll), 1939-
    Angry like Jonah: when God's children
throw tantrums

    1. Bible—O.T. Jonah.   2. Anger.   3. Jonah.
I. Title.

            152.47

ISBN 0-8280-1296-2

DEDICATED

with love and special thanks to Joann, for your childhood
fascination with Jonah without which this book would not be.
And to Jon, for your questions that still push me
to think beyond that which I already know.

CONTENTS

A WORD FROM THE AUTHOR

Swallows skim the water, a heron fishes among the lily pads, mists drape the hills, and a paddle length away a bass swirls the lake surface. As the canoe carries me through this tranquil setting, my mind searches for the right words. I have much I want to say. You see, although one individual may write a book, it is often a synthesis of ideas and information belonging to many others. It is particularly true of this book. I think of insights I've gleaned from the works of Ron and Nancy Rockey, Paul Hegstrom, Arlene Taylor, and Graham Maxwell. I think of the individuals who have allowed me to tell their stories. And I think of my soul sister Toini Harrison, who so generously shared time and materials. (She also has the knack for getting me to laugh my way through that malady known as writer's block.) Above all, I think of my dear husband, Date. His encouragement, abounding wisdom, amazing sense of humor, readiness to read the manuscript and suggest improvements, and daily prayers for the Lord to be with me as I write have all made producing this book much easier.

But writing a book takes more than ideas, information, and encouragement. It also needs time and space.

As missionaries, Date and I travel frequently, and this book has taken shape in various places in Europe, Canada, the United States, and Africa. In March 1997 war forced my evacuation from our mission in Lubumbashi, Zaire. Date, as ADRA director, stayed behind. And as before when I had to leave because of military unrest, family and friends opened their hearts and homes. Dad and Bernice made sure I had a place to go and a way to get there, my brothers, Wes and Greg, took me out for a spot of fishing, Alice Schultz sent over those luscious cinnamon buns, and others, too many to name, extended love and friendship in many ways.

9

Now that the war is momentarily over, Date has come to join me. In a few weeks we will return to our mission home in the country that now calls itself the Democratic Republic of the Congo. As the canoe carries me through the dawn and into the fullness of morning, I think of all this and praise the Lord for His love, His goodness, and the generosity of others. Even the canoe is not our own. And as I turn it toward the beautiful lakeside home so generously made available for our use by Emmet and Annette Koelsch, I know that we can never adequately express the magnitude of our appreciation, that I must content myself with conveying what I feel in a few simple words.

So to each of you, my heartfelt thanks.

Corrine Vanderwerff
Silver Lake, Washington

THE SIGN OF JONAH

"No sign will be given . . . except the sign of Jonah," Jesus told the unbelieving Jews who pushed Him for a sign from heaven (Matt. 12:39; 16:4; Luke 11:29). "For just as Jonah became a sign to the people of Nineveh, so the Son of Man will be to this generation (Luke 11:30). For just as Jonah was three days and three nights in the belly of the sea monster, so for three days and three nights the Son of Man will be in the heart of the earth. The people of Nineveh will rise up at the judgment with this generation and condemn it, because they repented at the proclamation of Jonah, and see, something greater than Jonah is here!" (Matt. 12:40, 41; see Luke 11:32).

JONAH AND JOANN

I'm angry. Angry enough to . . ." The girl's words suddenly stopped, and her taut facial muscles slackened into lines of worry. "I . . ." A moment's hesitation. "I know God will send me to hell for feeling like this. But . . ." A quick shrug spoke hopelessness at trying to change the situation.

The struggle against anger is nothing new. God's first recorded words after banishing Adam and Eve from the garden are His question to Cain: "Why are you angry?" Judging by faces we see on the street and those pictured in the popular media, the question is even more appropriate today. Yet many, convinced that being Christian and being angry are mutually exclusive, fear eternal damnation because of the anger they feel. Back in Bible times the prophet Jonah's anger got him into one of the most unusual predicaments of all time.

When Joann, our firstborn, was 2 going on 4 and brother Jon too young to comment, she and we had an ongoing ritual. "What story would you like tonight?" her daddy would ask when he came to wish her a good night.

Her answer never varied. "Jonah."

Never mind that at tuck-in time she and Mommy had already

11

held a similar conversation. "What story would you like tonight?"

"Jonah."

And at each bedtime she heard, as many times as she could, about the boat and the big wind and the big waves and the big fish and the prophet who had tried to run away from God. Even her biggest and most-loved dolly carried that favored name—Jonah.

Jonah knew about Nineveh, the place God wanted to send him. He also knew about God. And what he knew did not add up to his concept of justice. So when God said "Go!" he ran. In the opposite direction, toward Spain, to get as far from Nineveh—and God—as his world would allow. That's when God sent the storm and the fish.

For Joann, the ending of her Jonah story was happy. The big fish left the runaway prophet on dry land, and he picked himself up and went and did what God had asked. After all, happiness and blessings do result naturally when one does as told, don't they? And the rest of the story does show Jonah's outstanding success as a preacher, results that would make any evangelist proud. The king and the people, and even their cows and sheep and goats, wore sackcloth and fasted. And the king and the people repented and prayed for God's forgiveness.

But for Jonah . . .

"I knew it!" he yelled at God when the allotted 40 days had gone by and the city and the people remained untouched. "That's why I ran in the first place! You're too kind. Too ready to change Your mind. Too . . ."

To top it off, his plant suddenly wilted. Just like that. Without warning. His shade plant! Shriveled and useless! Leaving him sitting out in the burning sun! After all his hard work that was the final straw, and the last we see of him he's bawling full-temper toward the heavens. "I'm angry—angry enough to die!" (see Jonah 4:9).

Jonah's fury about the way God handled things seemed an inappropriate ending for our little Joann, so we stopped her bedtime story at the upbeat point where the prophet decides to obey. Many retellings of the Jonah story stop there. That's possibly part of our problem. Not only have we been selling both Jonah and God short; but we've been cheating ourselves and even our children of the deeper insights that the rest of the story leads us to consider. Though the story doesn't tell us outright that Jonah changed, God has the last word, and the fact that the story is in the Bible indicates that God's answer touched home. You see, God calls us to share the understandings He has given us. That's why Jonah had the courage to tell what happened. And that's why I'm writing this book.

The underlying reasons of Jonah's anger, and what happened because of it, make his story particularly meaningful for the growing numbers of Christians today who are discovering that they are not only angry, but angry at God.

JONAH AND ME?

Jonah? Good story.

Only fellow I know of who was swallowed by a fish and lived to tell about it.

Jonah . . .

and *me?*

What?

Are You trying to say . . . ?

No.

Impossible.

There can't be any connection.

Jonah was a prophet way back in Bible days. I'm just an everyday, next-door Christian. You called him, talked to him directly, tried to send him on a mission to Nineveh. But You've never talked to me like that. Besides, Jonah was as headstrong as they come. Thought he could outrun You. Why in the world You ever bothered with that hot-tempered, self-willed egotist I certainly cannot fathom.

CHAPTER 1

THE OTHER SIDE OF THE RIVER

Rob leveled the Cessna and leaned forward, peering through the window. The engine's roar pulsed against my ears. Below us the wing's shadow clipped across clumps of the coarse-green, thirsty-looking grass bordering a naked stretch of dust-brown earth. I had not planned to be aboard. Not now. A week in this isolated African village did not fit my schedule. But JeanLuc, principal of the project school, had arrived at our mission office about the time the school year should have started. He was even thinner than usual.

"I'm not going back!" His brown eyes had snapped with anger. "I'm not!"

At about the same time I'd been idea-storming, as we writers tend to do from time to time, and a catchy paragraph about the prophet Jonah began flowing onto my computer screen. "Did you ever find yourself where you didn't want to be?" asked the first sentence. "Jonah did. Suddenly scooped into the mouth of some swimming monolith! Flushed down its throat!" My nose wrinkled involuntarily. If I had been in his place, I'd have clawed for a hand-hold and fought to get myself out. My skin crawled as I imagined his hands slipping along warm, slimy membrane.

"Inside a fish! Incredible!"

The story transcends discussions of scientific feasibility. A mira-

15

cle is a miracle. Whether you take it as fact or as allegory, the plot deals with Jonah's relationship with God. When God called, Jonah ran. For that, God gave him a three-day time-out, as the Hebrews counted time, and for those three days it was just Jonah and the fish.

"Jonah? JeanLuc?" My writer's instinct suggested that a parallel ran through the two stories. Now I leaned against the plane's window. Below us and to the right, ragged palms and tangles of brush marked the limits of the unkempt countryside through which the villagers had hacked out the airstrip. Rob held us to a low pass, winging straight and steady, his eyes reading the beaten earth surface. It had been more than a year since a plane had landed there.

"Hey!" a part of me wanted to shout. "We've come this far; we've gotta give it a try."

We had come a long way. At least I had. The distance, though, reached far beyond the three-plus hours it had taken us to fly from mission headquarters to this lonely village, spanning more than miles and continents and oceans. Fortunately the sensible part of me withheld comment. In fact, that part of me did not particularly care to land even if the strip were safe. I felt like a Jonah strapped in the Cessna's belly, being carried toward a mission I did not want. I doubted that my wisdom, tact, and patience were equal to dealing with the situation created by the problem of JeanLuc.

With his Christian zeal, teaching experience, talents, keenness for evangelism, common tribal roots, and knowledge of the local language, JeanLuc appeared to be a God-given candidate to head the Christian school and development project my husband had initiated in this isolated area. When JeanLuc arrived, the people had welcomed him with open arms, giving him a house and organizing temporary quarters for a school. They also cleared land and prepared fields so that they and their youngsters could learn the new gardening techniques he'd promised to teach, and they had started making bricks for new school buildings and a church. Under JeanLuc's guidance, success for the project seemed inevitable. Then one night the little people came. Dwarfs. Appearing out of nowhere, just like that, running back and forth through his house. Night after night they materialized.

"Papa!" His children's eyes were round with fright.

"Do something," his wife begged.

JeanLuc prayed with his family, then went to see the chief. The little people disappeared, but just when JeanLuc dared hope they'd gone for good, they came back.

"Because I'm from the other side of the river," he told us.

For JeanLuc that statement explained not only the phantoms, but all the bad things that started happening to him. Would-be project directors and schoolteachers were jealous, he said, and they began making up stories about him. They said he stole the money meant to buy books for the school, that he had sold the children's uniforms and pocketed the money. People said that he kept the produce from the gardens meant for the children. And they even accused him of trying to poison the chief, to kill their paramount leader with the magic of witchcraft. That's why they paid their own wizards to scare him and his family away with the nighttime phantoms.

From the first, JeanLuc determined to keep the project going. And in spite of everything, he stayed on. Then one night, long after darkness had fallen, a gang carrying hoes and machetes pushed along the moonlit road. Shouting and singing crude lyrics, they marched through the opening in the hedge and up the path to his house. Banging on the door, they shouted more threats. The children huddled in the back room with their mother. JeanLuc peered through a corner of the window.

"There was even a man with a gun." His eyes were round as he told his story, as if he still could not believe what he'd seen. "If it hadn't been for Ilunga Ngoyi . . ."

Ilunga Ngoyi. One man against an angry mob. When he spoke, though, they listened. After all, he was their best football player, and when he ordered the ruffians on their way, they went. That night he smuggled the family into hiding and then secretly sent them in a dugout canoe across the river to the safety of the other side.

"But never come back," he warned.

"I can't go back," JeanLuc said.

Everyone agreed on that point. There was too much anger in the village.

"Because I'm from this side of the river."

The river cuts between people with a common language and with common tribal roots. In the past it had served as the road over which war parties stealthily paddled at night, landing up-river from opposing villages, creeping through the forest, then attacking and plundering. The one side against the other. Even in times of outward peace, old hatreds and accumulated anger did not completely disappear. JeanLuc, intruder from the other side, had been gaining the trust and respect of too many children. Even of their parents. That, according to the more traditional villagers, must be stopped.

"Lies!" JeanLuc shouted the day he arrived at the mission, holding out a copy of a letter of accusation that someone had carefully let fall into his hands. "Lies! Nothing but lies! I . . . I . . ." His mouth opened and shut again soundlessly, and his hands trembled.

"It's all right, brother." The person across from him spoke quietly, holding his hands up as if to soothe the irate outburst.

"I've had enough!" JeanLuc found his voice again, and the words snapped out. "I'm angry! Very angry! And I want them . . ."

Suddenly he stopped midsentence and abruptly sat down, dropping his head into his hands. And there he sat.

Have you ever found yourself in a position similar to JeanLuc's—target of too much, your words splaying left and right like bullets? Have you ever found yourself wishing for justice, fiery justice, to fall on your tormentors? Jonah did, and by the end of his story he had made a fool of himself.

Recent generations of Christians have been taught that anger is wrong. They've been told to sit on their anger, to repress it, and woe to the one who lets fly angry feelings. After all, Jesus did say that if someone wrongs you or slaps you on the face, you should simply turn the other cheek (see Matt. 5:39; Luke 6:29). The Bible also tells us that the "one who is slow to anger is better than the mighty" (Prov. 16:32). The biblical case against uncontrolled anger is strong. On the other hand, the Bible also talks about God Himself being angry. Defenders of Scripture quickly explain that God's anger is holy. Ours isn't. Yet we've been taught that we're created in His image and that we are to reflect His glory. Where does anger fit in?

When you *blow your stack*, or *fly off the handle*, or *lose your cool*, or otherwise explode into a violent outburst of what is generically known as *anger*, you are usually quite aware that your behavior is anything but Godlike or holy. And you wonder if there is such a thing as holy anger. After all, popular psychological theory encourages us to express our anger. "Let it all hang out," therapists say, because buttoning up your feelings or zipping your mouth can lead to repressed anger. And you wonder if they don't have a point because repressed anger quickly proves itself to be unhealthy and self-defeating. Hurting the angry one and not the one at whom the anger is directed can cause headaches, low back pain, nightmares, and depression. It shows up in sour, complaining, critical attitudes. Repressed anger produces Christians who do not reflect the spirit of Christ. On the other hand, expressing anger is not Christlike because it hurts others. And we stand between two bad options, searching for a good answer.

Many self-help books give good step-by-step processes for dealing with anger. But helpful as they are, such volumes talk mainly about alleviating symptoms and seldom reach to the deeply hidden root cause. Some individuals go to the Bible for further help and become disappointed when answers don't jump off the page with a quick 1, 2, 3 solution that says "Do this, and you'll never be angry again." The Bible does point the way toward recovery from the problems of anger, though, and it shows how to obtain deep healing. Part of the reason that we do not recognize or understand the aid it offers is that few of us have learned to distinguish between the feeling of anger and the expression of angry feelings. There is a difference. The story of Jonah offers an excellent starting place for understanding the difference and for finding how you can have healing in your own life.

JONAH AND GOD

"Now the word of the Lord came to Jonah son of Amittai, saying, 'Go at once to Nineveh, that great city, and cry out against it; for their wickedness has come up before me.'"

—Jonah 1:1, 2

Can You imagine?

A message from You saying "Go! Tell your enemies that I'm fed up with their wickedness."

And Jonah dared to disobey.

If I'd have had an order like that . . .

What?

How can You say that?

Me? Refuse?

A direct message?

No. Never.

I'd be too scared to disobey.

Pardon me?

Why was I having second thoughts in the plane?

But that's different. I . . .

CHAPTER 2

NEVER TO NINEVEH

B ecause I'm from the other side of the river," JeanLuc had said when he ran. The reasoning could have worked equally well for Jonah. God had originally set the northern boundary of Israel at the Euphrates, and Nineveh was far beyond that great river. "Go to Nineveh? That terrible place?" Back then, during the eighth century before Christ, Jonah had tried to twist sense out of the idea. "Me? A God-serving prophet of modern-day Israel? Me? Cross the river and preach? Surely not!"

Jonah's thoughts suddenly became alive with the beauties and comforts of his hometown. He'd been so convinced that it was where he belonged—for always. Convinced that he was doing what he should be doing and doing it where he should be doing it. "They need me here!"

Gath-hepher, the place of the winepress. Home. His people had not known such prosperity since the golden days during the reigns of the great kings David and Solomon. Even the boundaries of the country were where they belonged, thanks to King Jeroboam II's military accomplishments.

"Just as I predicted!" (see 2 Kings 14:25).

After his prophecy that the king would restore the borders of Israel, events made it look as though they might regain prominence as a nation to be reckoned with—under the right guidance, of course.

Jonah smiled now and slid his hands into the folds of his shirt. "A fortunate town, this," he mused. "Not many such these days with a reputable resident prophet!" He chuckled to himself. "Prophet Jonah!" Those words did have a special ring to them. Sort of musical. Inspiring. "A name that can be trusted." Chuckling again to himself, he looked up the street, then down. The other men were, without a doubt, away on business or over at the city gate. He nodded thoughtfully. "And I do predict even better times ahead. If God . . ."

Suddenly his contentment lurched. When Moses had begged to see God, God had passed before him and shown His goodness. "His goodness," Jonah repeated, remembering the off-quoted, much-loved description God had given of Himself to the beloved leader of His people. "The Lord, the Lord God," God had said, "merciful and gracious, longsuffering, and abundant in goodness and truth, keeping mercy for thousands, forgiving iniquity and transgression and sin" (Ex. 34:6, 7, KJV).

"Forgiving?" Instead of having a cheerful ring, the word weighed on his tongue, heavy, tasting like brass. "Nineveh?" His breath caught in his chest, and he slowly turned his head as if looking for something, anything, that he could use to deny the idea forming in his mind. "God in His mercy might forgive the Ninevites?" Them? Those savages! The very idea was . . . was . . .

"Im-pos-si-ble!"

The word hissed off his tongue, and his thoughts began spinning, reeling through ancient stories of God's threats against the Israelites when they had gone their own headstrong ways, when they'd let themselves be tempted into the forbidden cultic orgies. Women and men enticed into the groves by the shrine prostitutes. And the sacrifices. Their very own children placed into the blazing arms of the old Canaanite gods. When God warned of terrible things to come and the people repented, God had . . . had . . .

"Changed His mind?"

Jonah sat down. Hard. On his bench. Not wanting to comprehend what his own good sense was telling him about the mercy of his God.

God!

And Nineveh?

His thoughts spun round and round.

Upside down.

Inside out.

To Nineveh!

God wants

me

to go

to

Nineveh!

Me?

The longer he considered the call, the more the words chiseled themselves against the far wall of his mind.

To the Ninevites?

Assyrians, they were.

Marauders.

Dragging away captives from Israel.

Innocent women.

Children.

Elders.

The gentle.

The kindly.

Noses chopped off.

Ears hacked away.

Tongues torn out.

He'd heard about those tortures

—and worse.

Carved pictures, even,

showing them in gross detail

decorated Nineveh's walls.
And taxes.
Nineveh's kings
and their pagan gods
reclined
in palaces dripping with gold,
in palaces wasteful with wealth
stripped from Israel.
Jonah's blood boiled.
Go to Nineveh?
Risk God's mercy?
Toward them?
Never!

He sprang to his feet, ran into the house, pulled out his leather traveling belt, and rummaged through it. Money bag. Dried nuts. Dagger.

"Good!"

He strapped it over his ankle-length garment, stuffed some raisin cakes and dates into a bag, tossed on his wool cloak, grabbed up his walking staff, and strode out the door.

"Enough of this Nineveh business."

His steps, hard and determined, carried him southward along the road toward Joppa.

CHAPTER 3

BECAUSE

Jonah slung one foot ahead of the other in quick, long strides, looking neither to the right nor to the left. "Expecting me to . . ." His jaws clenched together, tooth set against tooth, and his facial muscles tensed until they were taut and rigid. "He . . ."

Though Jonah's posture spoke pure anger, his admission of it did not come until much later. That's the way it is for many. They are incapable of naming their real feelings. In addition, they *know* that whatever the problem is, they themselves are not at fault, that they are not to blame for their powerful negative emotions.

Growing up as I did on a secluded farm, I was ecstatic when Cousin Freddy and his brother, sisters, and parents arrived for an extended visit. It was like being in heaven to have other kids to do kid things with. We played hide-and-seek, hiked the wooded hills, searched for gold in the rocky creek (the most precious mineral we found was a rusted tin can), and listened in the evenings while the adults swapped stories. Then one day I discovered my little wooden puppet dog lying on the shelf, his knobby body sagging unnaturally. Grabbing him up, I rushed off to find Cousin Freddy.

"Look!"

I shoved the dog toward his face and punched at the button under its red stand. Instead of bowing and bobbing and barking in a happy, high-pitched squeak, as he always had, the dog fell forward into a loose cluster of beads, his little wooden head with its black leather ears dangling from the end of too much string. "What did you do?" I demanded. "Squeaker doesn't bark!"

Cousin Freddy shrugged.

"You broke him." Cousin Freddy had a reputation, and it did not take a detective to know that he and he alone was responsible for the deplorable condition of my toy.

"I wanted to see what made him work."

Cousin Freddy sounded as though the world was still perfectly fine. It wasn't. My little Squeaker dog was broken. My chest tightened. "You took it"—I planted my right foot a half-step closer to the boy—"without asking."

Cousin Freddy fished in his pocket, seeming not to have registered a word I had said. "See!" He pulled out a round cardboard-looking something and held it out on the palm of his hand. "I found it in there." He pointed at the little red box. "That's what makes it bark!"

"Put it back!" I ordered.

"Can't. It won't go."

"Fix it!"

"I can't!"

"You have to."

"Can't."

I may as well have been shouting at the wall. "Then I'm gonna tell!" Turning, I stomped down the stairs. "Mom! Look what Freddy did!" I thrust the toy toward her—she'd bought it for me when I'd been hospitalized during a long bout with pneumonia the previous year. "Make him fix it!"

She took the dog and looked it over, then shook her head.

"Mom!"

"He just wanted to see how it works."

"He broke it. Make him fix it."

"I can't."

"Mom!"

"It can't be fixed."

My ears heard, but my mind refused to accept the meaning of her words, and my "kid heaven" burst with the explosion of my 8-year-old sense of justice. "I want my dog!" Tears rimmed my eyes. "He broke it on purpose!"

Her lips firmed. "It can't be fixed," she repeated.

Something hot seemed to be squeezing around my throat. "Then spank him!" The words forced out in tight squeals. "Spank him!" My temples throbbed. I wanted justice where justice was due. "On his bottom!"

Mom started talking about boys, and healthy curiosity, and—

But my mind was full of only one thought. "Spank him!" I screeched.

Suddenly I was on my way to my room. For screaming. *Me!* When Freddy had broken *my* dog.

Our mothers organized an exchange of "I'm sorry's" that we dutifully mouthed. In due time Cousin Freddy did grow into a fine man whose technical curiosity led him into a good career, and the episode of the dog faded into those annals that, when retold, do nothing more than raise a chuckle about the times when we were kids. Yet the story provides an ideal study of the anatomy of anger. From my childish viewpoint, these were the facts:

I wanted justice.

For completely clear reasons.

Therefore, whatever I felt had nothing to do with me.

What had happened was all Cousin Freddy's fault.

He had taken the dog.

He had broken it.

Unnecessarily.

Had he fixed it, all would have been forgotten.

But he didn't fix it.

He couldn't.

No one could.

And no replacement was available.

I wanted my dog.

I had a right to my dog.

That right had been violated.

By Cousin Freddy.

I was frustrated and hurt, but most of all, I was angry. Angry at Cousin Freddy.

Anger, that passion of displeasure resulting from injury, mistreatment, or opposition, usually shows itself in a desire to get back at the supposed cause of the feeling. Or to take flight from the situation. In this instance, I considered it my due to fight back, to make Cousin Freddy pay for what he had done. I wanted justice—immediate and painful—brought down on his bottomside, where, in my viewpoint, it would have the best impact. You see, he had told me that he wanted to see what made my little dog bark. He always wanted to see what made things work. I had told him in no uncertain terms that he was not to touch my dog. But he did. And he broke it. So obviously it was all his fault that I was angry. Because . . .

When one is angry, becauses come easily.

"Because Freddy broke my dog."

"Because I'm from the other side of the river."

"Because . . ."

Whatever the reasons given, the *becauses* tend to shift blame away from the one who is angry and onto the something or someone else viewed as being responsible for that anger. In my righteous opinion, blame for the broken dog and therefore for my feelings of anger lay squarely and solely upon Cousin Freddy. Even JeanLuc's becauses could extend to include those who had called him to cross the river. They should have known better than to send him on a mission to the other side. Look what happened. Obviously the Christian leaders—and God—had made a serious mistake. They were to blame. It is the way it has been since the beginning of sin.

Adam blamed Eve (and the God who had created her), Eve blamed the serpent (and by implication the God who created it), and the serpent (Satan) blamed God.

Blame-shifting had originated with Satan himself back in hidden eternity, when as Lucifer he became enraged because he imagined himself slighted by God. He started stirring up discontent among the other heavenly beings. "God is not fair!" he whispered. The accusation spread until everyone became involved in a heavenly war that soon centered in our world (see Rev. 12). "God is not being fair with you." The charming prevarication the serpent offered Eve implied the charge (see Gen. 2:15-17; 3).

God remains the number one target of our anger. Jonah's becauses also pointed back at God. "God is not fair in asking me to go to Nineveh," he could very well have said.

As well as being dangerous for him to go to Nineveh, it was out of place, even contradictory, to what the Israelites had always been taught. God had warned them to stay clear of their pagan neighbors. Under no circumstances were they to mix into the cultic orgies. The God of Israel was the one and only, the all-powerful, the Creator of heaven and earth. A jealous God. But compared to the action up in the pagan groves, His sacrifices and His Sabbaths and His ceremonies could be summed up with one word—*boring!* The people easily fell under the spell of their neighbors' handsome young priests and beautiful priestesses.

"God wants me to go? And if I go . . ." Others, he reasoned, could very well twist that into an excuse for their own waywardness. Besides, what justice would there be in stretching the Scripture's concept of loving aliens (see Lev. 19:34) to include the Ninevites?

"Unthinkable!"

With a quick shrug, Jonah squared his shoulders and hurried on his way.

JONAH AND FREEDOM

"Jonah set out to flee to Tarshish from the presence of the Lord."

—Jonah 1:3

Running away from people is one thing. But running away from God?

Imagine, a prophet running away from his God. How could that be possible?

Pardon me? I don't understand. What do You mean, he was free to choose? Wasn't he Your prophet?

CHAPTER 4

A PLACE WITH A FUTURE

Back at the village Rob suddenly banked the plane up and around, giving us a view of the large, mirror-gray lake. For a crazy instant Jonah slipped back into my mind. Nothing unusual. That's the way my writing ideas grow—in fragments and pieces.

"Would you look at that!" Unspoken, the exclamation burst through my thoughts as the plane banked back toward the airstrip. That thought had nothing to do with Jonah. I reacted the same way on every flight when the plane's window framed the village. Straight avenues. Wide boulevards. Trees. Cozy thatched houses. The neat green-and-brown layout looked like no other African village that we knew. "A place with a future!" is what Date had said from the very beginning. Who could have thought that mysterious nighttime apparitions, terrifying little people, could run through houses in such a tranquil setting. And now Rob was signaling a thumbs-up. We could land!

We zoomed toward the runway, and I could see people waving. The village from which JeanLuc had been forced to run? "Though by no choice of my own!" he said, for from the beginning he had decided not to be frightened away by anyone, not even by the phantoms. Instead of setting about to win over his accusers, though, he began surrounding himself with allies who, for one reason or another, sided against those who threatened him. Feelings mounted. Both sides insisted that they alone were right. Both sides quit working on the new school building. And both sides refused to yield—until the night of the mob.

After JeanLuc left, his replacement struggled to motivate the villagers to cross the invisible barrier separating one side from the other. "Everything is fine," he wrote to our office, repeating the same phrase he used since JeanLuc's departure. Then he added, "But please send someone to encourage the people to begin working together again. Otherwise, we can't finish the school buildings before the rains start."

Someone did need to go. Mission Aviation Fellowship (MAF) had a flight passing near there and would take passengers in—if it was possible to land. Date is development director for our mission, and the project was under his jurisdiction. Although I'm a full-time writer, I was also managing the child-sponsorship part of our projects. Date could not get away for the week, and I was immersed in my writing. However, sponsors needed updated photos of their children and reports. Taking pictures and collecting reports was part of my responsibility. Pierre came from that area. He knew the background of the situation and the people. In addition, he had a knack for putting us in contact with the right individuals. If Pierre would come . . .

So I agreed to go.

When the plane trundled to a stop at the end of the runway, people flooded toward us, smiling, waving, shouting. We climbed down onto the patch of unoccupied grass they'd left around the plane.

"Lolo Kayumba!"

I smiled back at the one calling to me.

"Lolo Kayumba!"

The name repeated itself on many sides, and I felt drawn into the festive mood created by all the laughing and cheering voices. "Hear that!" I started to turn, to point to all the people. "That's my name! Lolo Kayumba! They gave it to me." I looked around.

Rob had already gone—he needed to walk the strip, to check it and leave instructions for its upkeep before he flew on. Pierre too had disappeared.

"Lolo Kayumba! Welcome!" Outstretched hands motioned to me.

Stepping toward them, I clasped several in a series of quick greetings. In the next instant a waist-high wall, solid and living, crushed around me. I felt my body being squeezed upward until my toes barely scraped the ground. Small hands, dozens of them, clutched at my arms.

"Lolo Kayumba!"

I looked down. Faces, dusty and smiling, crowded around me—more faces than I could count. Ragged shirts and blouses pulled across skinny shoulders, and dark eyes looked up, innocent of the problems that had brought us.

This mass of children.

Children from the project schools.

Children of the little people.

Children influenced by forces I did not understand.

Crushing through each other.

Reaching out to touch . . .

"Me!"

Wow! I really had come a long way!

And for a brief moment I remembered my own younger self, a self that contrasted sharply with these youngsters. The self I remembered was bulky, dressed in sloppy plaid shirt and worn jeans, hunched on a stool, head pushed against Mollie's comfortable flank, aiming milk into the bucket clasped between chubby knees. I was alone then. Always alone. Not just on the farm. But at school. Everywhere. My world back in those days had already focused inward.

"I . . ."

Tears came in private.

"I . . ."

Only the ears of Mollie the cow heard my vows.

"I'll show them!

"I'll be someone!

"I'll go places!

"I . . ."

Why things went so badly for me then, I didn't know. I'd grown up beside a river and had crossed it to attend a Christian school. The other youngsters came from homes that held the same beliefs as mine. Therefore, the fact that I lived on the other side of that river should have made no difference between me and the others. Yet somehow it did, and I had grown up angry because I had not really belonged. It wasn't my fault that I had been so unusually big and . . . But that was long ago and far away, and since then I had gone many places, and now here I was in Africa, a missionary visiting one of *my* villages.

If they *could just see me now!* I was thinking. (The *they* included everyone who'd distanced themselves from me when I was growing up.) I slipped my arm free from too many tugging grasps and reached out to touch more hands. The years had changed my circumstances almost more than even I could believe. I had friends, good friends, in many parts of the world, and here I was being mobbed by thousands of kids. The kids crowded in, impatient to be able to tell their own little world that they'd actually touched the White woman from America, the one who'd come in the airplane, the director of their project, the one known by the African name they had given her, their own Lolo Kayumba. That they had touched . . .

Me!

As I reached toward another eager hand, a youngster to my left shrieked. That's when the wave of bodies hit.

I stumbled sideways.

Hands grabbed my arms. Tugging.

I swayed. This way. That. Unable to fall. Unable to stand. Unable to do anything except to let myself be bobbed about, a White woman sticking at undignified angles out of a solid mass of little dark heads and shoulders.

When I tried to call for help, I instead tipped further. A startled

"Uh!" squished out of my mouth, and I started sinking. The inevitable feet were getting closer. I struggled. The only direction I moved was down! Then my feet dropped. Solid ground! I pushed upright, grabbed shoulders, twisted around, levered my back against the thinnest layer, and shoved. A space snapped open. With a lunge I landed on an empty patch of grass, leaving the children to flow back into their original groupings.

Like the children, compacted by those pushing in from the outer edges, anger usually rushes in on us like a single, overpowering unit. Yet psychologists tell us that the package we normally call anger is actually more than a single emotion. Anger never exists by itself. It is always preceded by one or another of a dozen or more different emotions or feelings. For example, my sense of loss and dejection about the irreparable remains of my toy dog and my frustration at my mother's apparent unwillingness to understand my grief provoked my rage against Cousin Freddy. Angry feelings flare so quickly, though, that unless made aware of the process, few people recognize the different emotions and feelings involved in causing their anger. The three most common primary emotions that precede anger are fear, frustration, and hurt. Feelings of disappointment, discouragement, confusion, shame, guilt, inadequacy, dejection, helplessness, hopelessness, and rejection can also trigger anger.

Analyze some of your own angry outbursts, and you may notice a progression. Once safely on the other side of the river, JeanLuc's feelings of helplessness, shame, and discouragement about what had happened were soon eclipsed by his anger at the way he had been treated. Jonah's frustration with the implications of God's call turned into a seething interior anger that caused him to run. Running away, though, did not solve his problem, and Jonah's angry outbursts were still to come. Awareness of and learning to deal with the particular feelings or combinations of feelings that precede or point toward your anger can help you avoid further outbursts.

CHAPTER 5

THE STORM

Tarshish," Jonah said when he found a ship about to sail. Then he mumbled something about "the end of the world because God . . ."

"People travel for the daftest reasons!" the captain exclaimed as the prophet clambered aboard. "As long as they pay their way and stay out from underfoot—" He waved his arm toward Jonah, signaling him aft toward a heap of bundles. "Why they're on board—that's their concern. Not ours."

Jonah did do his best to keep out of the way, and when they were well at sea, he settled in. There in the security of the ship's hold he relaxed. "Wise choice," he complimented himself. "Only sensible thing to do. Getting away like this. Beyond God's territory." The rhythmic dip of the oars, the gentle roll of the waves, and the wisping of the water against the hull soon lulled him into a deep, comfortable sleep.

"Hey, you!"

Jonah suddenly felt himself on the upswing of a strange roller-coaster dream.

"Sleeping? In this gale!"

Jonah twisted his head from side to side, then through bleary eyes saw the captain swaying over him.

"Get up!"

The boat heaved in another direction.

"Pray to your God!"

Jonah rolled with the pitch and began skidding along the suddenly sharp incline.

"Pray!"

The hull suddenly slapped upright, knocking him back in the direction from which he'd just come.

"Maybe your God'll save us!"

The boat held its balance momentarily, then pitched upward. By the time the next wave hit, Jonah had pulled himself to his feet, and groping along the uneven humps of cargo, he stumbled after the captain. On deck they found a huddle of sailors.

"We tossed . . ." The wind tore at their explanation, but Jonah could see fingers jabbing in his direction. The wind slacked momentarily, and in that instant one word blared clear. "You!"

A dull fear slapped over his back and clamped around his lungs and stomach.

"The lots fell . . ."

Calamities did not just happen. Everyone knew that. Someone always caused them. Of course, in their fear to protect themselves, the crew would be hunting out the guilty one, someone who had offended the gods.

"You! Why's this happening? Tell us!"

The pitching deck. The wild sea. Jonah reached out to steady himself. "I, uh . . ." he stammered. "Because. . ." He struggled to speak.

"Who are you, anyhow?" they demanded. "What's your occupation? your country? your people?"

Jonah did his best to make sense of their rapid-fire questions, to give coherent answers. Another wave slammed, this time broadside against the hull. He staggered.

"What shall we do?"

"Do?" Jonah's thoughts clawed through each other. "God?" Spray drenched his clothes, and the deck's sudden list threatened to throw him to his knees. "I . . ." He struggled to make his words loud enough. To make them make sense. "I'm running away from my God. The God of heaven. The God who made the earth and the sea."

The sailors had heard stories about the God of Israel. Centuries before, He'd pushed a path through the Red Sea for His people and then let the waters crash back down on the armies of pharaoh. Again some 40 years later He parted the Jordan at flood stage for them. Not many days after that, when they had laid siege to the great city of Jericho, He, through some heavenly magic, had toppled the heavily fortified walls. The sailors stared at this strange man. "Running away?" They could not understand. From such a God? A God who spares His people and destroys their enemies? It did not make sense.

"What'll we do?" Faces drained of their color, mouths forming and reforming the question, the men grappled to keep themselves upright, desperately begging one another for answers, for hope. Their own gods were unpredictable and unreliable, and sometimes demanded impossible sacrifices and penances to turn their fury. But the God of Israel, for no known reason, was punishing them. "What'll we do? How can we be saved?"

Even today many view themselves as victims of an indiscriminately cruel God, a God who, for no apparent good reason, is bent on punishing with fires, earthquakes, floods, hurricanes, and other cataclysmic disasters of unimaginable proportions. "Watch out," they warn, "or God'll get you!" And like the sailors, they look in every direction for protection from His vengeance.

Although Jonah, and with him the ship's crew, experienced a one-of-a-kind divine interaction, what happened next indicates how God meets people where they are and works through events for their eternal good. Educators call it redemptive punishment and corrective discipline. Jonah's hidden anger and warped relationship with God caused him to panic and run. God turned the prophet's disobedience into an opportunity to act out an object lesson that would reach beyond the prophet and his shipmates to include every ensuing generation. When the storm pivoted everyone's attention on Jonah, God stepped in again.

A new manliness surged through the prophet. He braced his feet. "Throw me overboard!" he shouted.

The sailors gasped. The gods frequently demanded human sacrifices. But this?

"Row harder," the captain commanded.

The men bent to their oars, straining to force the boat into the storm, toward land. Waves scooped higher. The bow flipped upward, and the forward oars flailed through open space. Crash! Heads snapped as they bottomed into the trough, and the hard seats cracked upward, jolting into their bodies. Water splayed heavenward. The wind grabbed the water, slapping it into jagged, clammy sheets, and throwing them over the oarsmen. Another wave loomed. Arrowlike, the bow rushed toward it. The men froze—helpless to staunch the avalanche poised above them. Then with a leap, their boat rode to the crest. Safe! For the moment, at least. Ashen faced, all turned toward Jonah.

"Impossible!" The idea froze in their minds. "A worshiper of that terrible God? A prophet? Into the sea? Kill him?"

"The storm will calm," Jonah insisted. "You're caught in it because . . ." He paused, stricken not by *what* was happening, but by *why* it was happening. "Because of me!"

"Row!" The captain's voice cut like a whip above their heads.

The men forced themselves beyond their strength. The storm worsened.

"Throw me overboard!"

They turned toward Jonah's voice. Waves towered over them.

"What a terrible thing to do! O Lord!"

Frightened prayers tore from their lips.

"Please! Not our lives for his!"

"You! And you!" At the captain's command, strong arms grabbed Jonah.

"Please! This is your doing!" The sailors hurled their pleas toward the angry, unseen God of the prophet, and quickly, before losing nerve, they flung the man up over the railing and into the storm. All eyes riveted on his plummeting form, watching as his robe billowed into a wide, woollen sail. An instant later a wave smashed around his body, gathering his robe into a sodden shroud, and the crest pummeled him under and down. Down.

"Look at that!"

Rounded eyes followed the direction of the pointing arm. Mouths gaped in astonishment.

"A fish?"

The sailors stood as though frozen, grasping the rail, staring into the water. The man was gone.

"O Lord!"

Then the wind dropped. Just like that. The waves settled. The crew looked at one another. At the captain. "That's what he said!" In awestruck tones they rehearsed what had happened. "He said, 'Throw me overboard and the storm will stop!'"

"His God has accepted him as a sacrifice."

"As payment for his sin."

"And we've been saved!"

"Did you see that?" A hand pointed toward a giant fin cutting the now-calm surface. "The fish!"

"Huge!"

Have-you-ever-seen-anything-like-it tones filled their voices. Replays of Jonah's answers and explanations scattered from man to man.

"A Hebrew."

"Worshiper of the God of heaven."

"The God who made the land and the sea."

"Even the very heavens!"

"A prophet—that's what he said."

"Called to Nineveh."

"Refused to go."

"How terrible!"

"His God sent the storm."

"A storm like that! Must be very angry."

"Imagine!"

"Such a powerful God!"

Heads shook.

"Running away!"

"Incomprehensible!"

"Prepare a sacrifice!" The captain's voice pulled them to attention. "To the all-powerful God of Jonah!"

Reverence and terror rested like a mantle over the rough sailors, and hasty promises sprang from their lips. "We'll always serve You!" And their eyes riveted on the faraway heavens. "Forever."

JONAH AND THE SAILORS

"But the Lord provided a large fish to swallow up Jonah."

—Jonah 1:17

All those sailors. Converted on the spot! You scored that time! And Jonah! His bravery. Seeing his mistake. Taking his punishment. Clearing his record, so to speak. Balancing the ledger. Wow!

What do You mean? The sailors weren't really converted? And Jonah didn't clear his record? I don't get it. Didn't they keep their promises? Didn't Jonah pay for his sin? Were You so angry that You wanted something more?

You say You're not angry? But . . . why the storm? If I'd been there, I'd . . .

You what? You want me to wait, to see what happens, and to think about it? Well, OK, but . . .

41

CHAPTER 6

INSTEAD OF ETERNITY

God! Help!" The wind wrenched Jonah's screaming prayer cry away, and a wave riding behind the others suddenly swelled into a gigantic rushing wall, wild and headstrong, surging higher and higher. An off-white froth streamed from its flanks. Its crest towered into a snarling foam mass dividing sea from heaven, tottering on unsteady footing. Then with a roar it fell into an avalanche of green-brown brine, untold tons of it, crashing down upon the plummeting prophet, slamming his body deep into the churning ocean.

Jonah clawed at the water, hands digging, desperately struggling to pull himself back toward the surface. His arms and legs flailed uselessly as he was jetted this way and that by the wrathful currents until they threw him like a bit of unwanted seaweed into a looping underwater spiral. His lungs screamed for air. His head felt like it was being crushed inward when a quick whoosh rolled him into a somersault, shooting him forward. Before he could turn himself, his body slammed against a solid something, rebounded, then settled. Stunned, he lay where he dropped. Gradually his senses began to return. He felt warm. Closed in. Drifting.

Drowning? Not so bad after all. But kinda cramped.

An eerie silence shut out everything but a dull ka-thud, ka-thud, ka-thud, that smacked rhythmically against his eardrums.

Pulse? For someone who's just drowned?

His chest rose and fell.

Breathing? No. Impossible. Must be hallucinating from the lack of air. Then . . .

Where's the water?

Why this feeling of being carried?

Things seem kinda stale, but rather nice. Graceful, fluid. Jonah relaxed into the motion, letting his body sag into the support upon which he lay.

Tired.

Time passed. His eyes opened. He blinked, and blinked again. Nothing but darkness. Too much darkness. Sticky and warm darkness. He pushed himself into a crouch and reached out one hand. And the other. Groping.

A wall? Walls? Flabby, sticky walls. All around.

Terror seized him. In that courageous moment back on the boat he'd thought it'd be only a few moments. That it'd all be over. And now . . .

It can't be! How'll I breathe? How'll I . . . No!

Not in his wildest imagination had he suspected the possibility of such an incredible turn of events. God had shocked others before. Moses with a flaming bush. Balaam with a talking donkey. Gideon with a disappearing visitor.

But a fish!

Instead of eternity?

"God! Let me out of here!"

But the fish swam on.

"And Jonah was in the belly of the fish three days and three nights."

—Jonah 1:17

CHAPTER 7

GOD SENT A FISH

Jonah's amazing rescuer carried the would-be runaway on a most incredible journey. Trapped, insulated from everything on the outside, it was just the prophet and the fish. Or was it? Sometimes we wish for similar protection from all that troubles us. A typical fall Northwest day stands out in my memory. Rainy. The teacher had just released us middle graders from a long, pent-up morning, and I bent over my school desk hunting for a book. Someone shoved against me. On purpose!

"Outta my way, Fatty!"

Pushing myself upright, I spun around.

"Ah-ha-ah-uh-haa-ha!" Freckles wagged his head in time to his chant, dancing like a cornered basketball player.

I glowered down at him. I was the tallest—and by far the widest—in our class.

"Fatty, Fatty, Fatty! Can't . . ."

A ball of resentment exploded. I lunged, full weight, on him.

Freckles lurched sideways, slamming against a desk, then bounced up immediately and again rocketed toward me. His hand flashed out. A row of desks, solid as a wall, blocked my attempt to jump out of his way. With a quick *rip* the bib of my cotton jumper hung in shreds. Freckles spun and hurtled on his way. The door slammed behind him, leaving me staring at my torn clothes, my head burning with what I wanted to have happen to him. "Mom!" I yelled, stomping into our kitchen eight minutes later. "Look!"

She did.

"Freckles did it! He always picks on me. They all pick on me!"

Mother listened, thin-lipped.

"Mom!" Tears stung my eyes. "Make 'em stop!"

I waited. Like I had the time when Freddy had broken the little dog. Hoping for her promise. Hoping to hear her say she'd take care of them, that she'd fix 'em good. But she said nothing. Not even the usual "Don't pay any attention to them."

"It's not fair!" My throat choked around the words. She had to understand—had to help. Somebody had to do something. "It's not fair!"

As I stared up at her, my ears burned with all the mean words I'd heard, a heavy ache churned in my chest and stomach. I willed her to say the magic words that would fix everything, that would turn my world into a happy place of acceptance.

Silence. And a simple shake of the head.

I didn't notice the sadness in her eyes then, because through that long pause flashed one of those bits of insight that come when youngsters are struggling across the threshold into the age of understanding. She couldn't help. I was backed against the wall of my world, and she couldn't do a thing. If I could have run away then, I would have. But I couldn't. Not physically. So I began to retreat into the world within my mind, unaware that the cause of my hurt had a name—rejection.

Rejection always hurts. During childhood, feelings of rejection can result from many things, ranging from the intentional rebuffs of classmates to the unavoidable extended absence of a parent. Clearly phrased and unmistakable words or an unspoken attitude can produce it. Whatever form rejection takes, it hurts. Recent findings by social scientists show that rejection actually is the worst of all forms of abuse. The effects of rejection are worse even than those of sexual, emotional, or physical abuse. Abuse of any kind,

45

though, leaves painful wounds within the victim and frequently provokes the wish to escape. Some choose to run, to get as far as possible from the cause of their hurt, and to create a new world for themselves. Most simply retreat into a protective inner world. Without my realizing what was happening, the rejection I perceived from my classmates put me on the first steps along that long, miserable road of being prisoner to my own sense of justice and fair play. I had no idea that the hurt I hid deep inside of me smoldered with anger and resentment.

Repressed anger tends to do that. It hides under other feelings such as hurt and self-pity. Or disappointment. Or jealousy and self-protectiveness. Especially self-protectiveness. When stresses mount, victims of repressed anger easily develop physical symptoms. They wonder why their joints, back or head aches. Others can't understand why they get migraines, or have recurrent night mares, or slip into continuing bouts of depression. When our Joann was 2 and fascinated with our bedtime version of the Jonah story, I strongly believed the moral I tacked on for her—that Jonah's punishment of being swallowed by the fish made him want to be good for ever after, and that if we do what God says, we'll be happy. The formula seemed simple. Pray. Try to be good. And everything will be fine. I prayed. I tried to be good. I even became a missionary. Yet for some reason, everything in my life was not fine. Then early in our stay in Africa I contracted a long-running, up-and-down bout with brucellosis (undulant fever). "You should listen to these," a friend in the mission office suggested on one of my better days. She pointed to a set of cassette tapes. "They're good. And they go through the Bible book-by-book."

I said something like "Sure, I'll try them sometime." The down days of brucellosis provided a good sometime. So I listened to them. They inspired me to explore the Bible on my own. That started me on an exciting path of discovery, but I preferred not to talk about certain things I was beginning to find within myself. They carried such labels as resentment and anger and self-pity. In the meantime, Joann had finished college and had married. By the time she was expecting her second child, I had long since recovered from the brucellosis. We scheduled our furlough so I could be with her when the baby came. Matthew, her 4-year-old, was fascinated with the little computer I brought along for my work.

"I'm writing a book about Jonah," I told him.

"But Grandma!" he exclaimed. "You can't do that!" He regarded me with his clear blue eyes. "Jonah's a kids' story! It's not a story for big people!"

Jonah's adventure with the boat and storm and fish does make a compelling kids' story. "It was your mommy's favorite when she was a very little girl." I smiled. He loved to hear about his mother when was she was little. "But big people like it too," I added.

Jonah is an excellent book. A narrative, scholars rank it among the best of the Old Testament writings. The prophet himself, though, scores very low. "Too proud and self-centered," they say. "An egotist. Willful, pouting, jealous, and bloodthirsty. Lacking proper respect for God and having no love for his enemies. Seething with resentment, anger, and self-pity."

Jonah did have a terrible personal profile. The scrolls of his time had all the truths necessary to instill a Godlike behavior, yet his childish self-will pushed him to run away from the very God he claimed to serve. Despite all of our modern sophistication, we can still learn from his experience. Our generation has more schooling, more information, and more books and instructional material than any previous one. We have more self-help materials than our parents had. Psychologists, therapists, and psychiatrists are at our beck and call. The spiritual have an abundance of Christian counselors, pastors, and religious teachers. Bibles are available everywhere. Yet with all the materials and help that we have at our disposal, we still do not know how to deal with our anger. Like Jonah, we blame anyone or anything other than ourselves for the problems we encounter. We talk about stress and financial problems and the abuses we suffered as children. Perhaps we take pride in calling ourselves *survivors*. Bemoaning the ineffectiveness of government and school and church in setting society straight, we see ourselves as innocent victims of a worsening socioeconomic environment.

When I was sick and unable to do anything but listen to the Bible tapes my friend lent me, I began to see life and God differently. Maybe God used Jonah's time in the fish to try to start him along a new track of thinking. Although the Bible does not directly say so, the possibility exists. At all times and in all ways, God endeavors to reach through to our understanding. Even in Jonah's time, God's people knew the Lord as the shepherd who cares. In Jonah's case, though, He sent a fish.

JONAH AND THE FISH

OK, I'm beginning to get it. Jonah was one of Your chosen men. Since he didn't go along with what You wanted, You gave him a time out, time to think. Yeah, I see. Like when You make people sick or make them go broke or cause them other trouble, so they can learn a lesson.

Pardon me? I might be right about him being able to use a time-out. But it wasn't Your idea to put him in a fish? And You aren't in the habit of making people sick or making things go wrong?

But I thought . . .

CHAPTER 8

GOD LOOKS AT THE HEART

Reddish-black flashes stabbed behind Jonah's eyes, a trick of his mind, a fantasy of the smothering blackness. He dug his fists in circular dabs against his eyelids, and twisted. It was hot, getting hotter. Night? Day? He had no idea. All he knew was . . .

"What a terrible thing to do!" His ears echoed with the sailors' last intelligible yells. "Terrible!" Again he felt himself being grabbed up like a sack of grain, slung by its corners between two burly seamen, and pitched up and over the side of the ship. It had happened so quickly that . . . He pushed out his hand now, then pulled it quickly away from the damp, rubbery surface. "No!" How could he dare believe his new horror? "Impossible!" And yet his senses insisted that this gross nightmare was reality. "A fish! God?"

His mind spun. "Take some olive oil." Disjointed sentence pieces whirled in and out of his consciousness. "Go." He tried to marshal them, to make them fit into sensible thoughts. Was the air running low? "Go? I . . . I'm sorry." Would he survive? "God, I . . ."

"Not you. Samuel."

His ears hummed.

"Get ahold of yourself!" Rolling his head from side to side, he felt hot. Feverish. "Think! Be logical! Now remember. I was on the ship. And . . ."

"Take some olive oil. Go."

49

"No! No!" He dug his fingers against his scalp. "Remember? That's a story from the scrolls. About Samuel . . . Samuel the prophet. When God told him to go to Bethlehem to anoint one of Jesse's sons to be the new king." Suddenly the details took form and became alive as if the old story were being acted out on the stage of his mind.

"Someone else to be king?" In his imagination he saw Samuel's face pale. "If Saul hears that, he'll . . ." Years earlier God had sent Samuel to anoint Saul to be the first king over their people. At the time God had filled Saul mightily with His Spirit. "He'll . . ."

"Go," God insisted.

"But Saul's still king!" Samuel had every reason to refuse God's order. Saul—tall, handsome, awesome in battle, a hero's hero, God's anointed. As such, he was worthy of honor. But the years had changed him. Unpredictable, that's what he'd become. Unpredictable, haughty, jealous. Easily angered, and that with a king's authority.

"He'll kill me!" Samuel lifted fearful eyes toward the heavens.

"Take a calf." God's order remained. "Tell them you've come to sacrifice."

And Samuel went.

He went! Jonah's conscience knotted.

"Aah! He must be the one." Samuel nodded toward the eldest of the brothers who had come to greet him in Bethlehem. "Tall. Handsome. Make a good-looking king."

Normal reaction. Jonah sided with Samuel. *God sends His prophets on such complicated errands, and . . .*

"Pay no attention to looks!"

God's interruption stopped Samuel's hand from reaching for his flask of olive oil and, instead, the prophet held out both hands toward Eliab, the eldest of Jesse's sons (1 Sam. 17:13) to welcome him to the sacrifice and to wish him a pleasant dinner.

Jesse brought six more of his sons and presented them to the prophet. Samuel, in his much-loved heartiness, greeted each in turn, then asked the father, "Don't you have any other boys?"

Jesse looked at his host. "There's the youngest." His voice held a questioning tone. *Since when did people concern themselves with the unimportant younger sons of a family?* "But he's off with the sheep."

"Call him!" Samuel replied. "We won't sit down till he comes."

The youngster they brought was good-looking enough, strong, healthy, and sparkly eyed. But . . .

So young?

"This is the one!"

Samuel muffled his surprise. "I don't judge as mortals judge." That's what God said when he wanted to anoint eldest brother Eliab. "Man looks at appearances. I look at the heart" (see 1 Sam. 16:1-13).

"Anoint him!"

Jonah had plenty of nothing to do but think.

God?

Why am I alive?

Here?

In this fish?

CHAPTER 9

HARD AS A BRICK

Jonah twisted and a moan slid through his throat, slithering around his head to vanish into the suffocating dankness. He rolled back to his other side. A spastic, gripping tightness reached across his back and along his legs. His stomach felt bloated and nauseous. A burning heat radiated from the base of his neck and along his shoulders. Mechanically, his hands fisted, and the sudden sharp biting of his fingernails into his palms pulled him to wakeful consciousness.

"I will harden Pharaoh's heart."

He groaned again, twisting his head around. Back and forth and back and forth he rocked his head, as if that might dislodge the relentless parade of disjointed bits from the scrolls.

"I will harden Pharaoh's heart."

Almost like a spoken voice, the sentence repeated itself. Suddenly Jonah's mind focused. He lay still. "If . . ." His heart quickened. "If God could make that wicked king stubborn and mean, then He could do the same to the Ninevites."

"No! No! And *no!*" Pharaoh's angry refusals echoed through his thoughts into a rhythmic chant, and again the prophet's mind became lost in the details of the story. When the plagues got too tough, Pharaoh would relent, and promise that the people could go—when the plagues stopped . . .

"No!" Pharaoh shouted again.

Release the Israelites? His slave workforce? Never! What could Moses and Aaron or their God do to him, anyway? As pharaoh he linked his people with the gods—in fact, he was a god himself! Let those hardheaded rebels leave? "Humph!" He had no intention of bowing to the desert god of a sniveling bunch of ragtag slaves. Not even when the Nile, Egypt's sacred river, thickened like blood. Not even when the air grew rank from the scent of crocodiles and fish rotting on her sacred banks. Not even when frogs, millions of them, hopped across the land. After all, it was not just Aaron's walking stick that had made the frogs come. No. His royal magicians had conjured up frogs too. Frogs lurked everywhere, croaking and hop-ping into the very pots and pans of the palace, and . . .

"Eeeyuck! Get these frogs out of my bed!" he bellowed at his servants. But no one could make them go away.

"Where's Heqet?" people began to whisper. Their frog-headed goddess, the goddess of creative power, seemed strangely silent about this invasion by her kind.

Finally Pharaoh relented and called for Moses.

Moses prayed. The frogs died. And while his servants were still scraping away the rotting, stinking carcasses, Pharaoh again turned brick stubborn—and angry.

"Refused!" Jonah could not understand. "In the face of those miracles? Even when his own magicians told him that the plagues were the finger of God" (Ex. 8:19).

"Why are you in this fish?"

"What's that got to do with Pharaoh? And frogs?"

"I sent the fish."

"But you got 'em! The Egyptians. In the Red Sea! Their army drowned. Our people were safe—on the other side, out of Egypt and on the way to the Promised Land. The whole world heard about Your power—how You hardened the great Pharaoh's heart and delivered Your people. Even the prostitute Rahab. She heard and

53

believed. And she hid our spies. For that You saved her. A prostitute. A pagan prostitute!" Jonah's rush of words suddenly slowed. "You punished Pharaoh. Saved a prostitute. And . . ."

"I saved you."

Jonah felt his world suddenly loop upside down, turn, then dip dizzily. *Me. Rahab. Pharaoh. Fishes and frogs.* The words swam through his head, out of order and mixed up again. Everything spun.

"Eeeyuck!" *Relax. Take a deep breath!* "Ohooohh!"

The fish swung another reckless loop, nosed upward, fast, then before Jonah's stomach could find its bearings, he found himself pitched downward. Instinctively he flopped his hands over his head as they plummeted.

Like a brick.

"Pharaoh's heart?"

By now his thoughts were totally confused.

"Eeeyuck!"

The fish continued to plummet.

"No! My stomach!"

Abruptly they leveled. Jonah's hands dropped to his side. His stomach floated back into place. His mind circled slower and slower. The story of Israel's deliverance—it did say that God had hardened Pharaoh's heart.

"Of course it did. Any good prophet knows that. Except . . ." *Why do I have to remember that now?* As a boy he'd questioned the story when he'd heard it read from the scroll. The same story. Saying different things. Saying that God had hardened Pharaoh's heart. Saying that Pharaoh's heart was hardened. Saying that Pharaoh had hardened his own heart. Three claims. Different and contradictory. All within the same scroll (see Ex. 8:32; 9:7, 12).

God. Satan. Pharaoh himself.

Jonah clamped his hands around his head and began rubbing his fingertips against his scalp.

"Of course, I should understand . . . I'm a prophet! That's the way we Israelites say things. God is one God, the God of everything."

Mentally he began stacking segments of the teachings one on top of the other. His people, the Israelites, weren't like the other nations that worshiped many gods, that credited this god with this and that god with that. They worshiped one God. The supreme God, Creator of heaven and earth. The God in charge of and responsible for everything. The same yesterday. Today. Forever. The source of all life. The God whose Spirit strives with every created being. Every one.

"Even Pharaoh?"

Jonah tried to reason it out.

God and Pharaoh? Yeah. God did send His Spirit to work on Pharaoh's heart. Pharaoh had wanted his own way. He had chosen—deliberately—not to listen to God's warning time after time. Choosing against God leaves only one other option. Choosing against God is choosing for . . .

The prophet's band of thoughts slid to a halt.

All good Israelites know there are only two choices. If you choose for God, then you automatically choose against the devil. But if you choose against God, then you automatically choose for . . . for . . .

He paused. Then slowly he looped through the details again. God sent Moses and Aaron to Pharaoh.

God sent His Spirit to Pharaoh.

God showed His power over Pharaoh's false gods.

And Pharaoh . . .

The harder God worked, the harder Pharaoh's heart became. He, *the pharaoh*, would not bow to another. He . . .

Jonah snorted. "God showed him, He did. Cut right through his arrogant, haughty, obstinate self-centeredness and showed him the worthlessness of his very gods—of Pharaoh's own godhood. Showed him you don't trifle with the real God. Showed him who's in charge. If I'd had to muck through all those frogs, I . . ."

"I asked you to go to Nineveh."

"But . . ." Jonah's thoughts slammed to a standstill, as abruptly as if the fish had plowed into the ocean floor.

JONAH AND GOD

Jonah's in some pickle. Can't you just hear him?
Pounding. Pounding on the fish's belly. Hammering out
his frustrations.

God?

Why?

Why couldn't I be an ordinary someone? Just
another common Jonah down the street? An average
Jonah with a few humble sheep? A simple Jonah without
a special mission?

Why, God?

Why this fish?

God?

CHAPTER 10

WHY?

W hy, Mom? Why?" Jon's blue eyes searched my face with the incredible trust in adult knowledge that comes when you're 4 going on 5. "Mom, why?"

"Because . . ." A few easy words formed the answer, but they did not stop the questions.

"Why, Mom?"

His whys developed a way of plowing far beyond my store of learning. And I'd have to shake my head. "Sorry, Jonny, but I don't know."

"But Mom! Why? Why don't you know?"

"I'm sorry. I just don't know the answer."

"But Mom!" His insistent treble carried us into a dialogue we'd been through a hundred times before. "Why?"

I'd shake my head again.

"But Mom! If you did know, what do you think the answer would be?"

"Huh?"

"If you did know . . ."

"Well . . ." A deep introspective breath. *If I did know, what do I think the answer would be? How am I supposed to answer these impossible questions and not dampen his enthusiasm to learn?* "I just don't know anything about it, so I can't even possibly think an answer now."

Then, brightening: "But maybe someday *you* can learn how to find the answer."

His quest for answers eventually led him into the world of mathematics and research. He learned how to find solutions for problems realms beyond the questions I'd found so impossible. Yet all the knowledge and all the problem-solving abilities in the world will not necessarily equip us with the ability to answer humanity's basic whys or to deal with our own tricky feelings. Nor do they automatically make us able to recognize the answers that God does provide for our questions.

Some 150 years after Jonah's encounter with the fish, the prophet Habakkuk hurled his own whys toward God. The Assyrians had long since carried the northern 10 tribes of Israel, Jonah's people, off to who-knows-where. The people of Judah apparently had not taken to heart any lessons from the catastrophic dispersion of their brothers and sisters to the north. Although priding themselves in being God's chosen, they continued to go their own self-pleasing ways. "Why don't You do something about all this wickedness around me?" Habakkuk pleaded with God.

Similar questions continue today. "God! Why did this happen? Why do the bad guys get the breaks? Why? Why the misery? Why do the innocent have to suffer? Why did this happen to me? Why, God? Why?"

Silence.

Deafening silence.

Hurt turns to anger, and white-knuckled fists beat the air. "If You are a God of love, why . . ."

"Watch," God told Habakkuk. "Trust Me. You're going to find this hard to believe, but I'm raising up the Babylonians" (see Hab. 1:2-11).

"The Babylonians? The pitiless Babylonian army?" God's answer made no sense to the prophet. "God, how can You stand by silent while the wicked destroy those who are better than they?"

"Write down My answer," God replied to His worried prophet. "Make it plain to everyone. If it seems slow, be patient. These things will surely happen at the right time. But the righteous will live by his faith" (see Hab. 2:4; Rom. 1:17; Gal. 3:11).

The Babylonians did come, terrible armies of them. They overran the country, destroyed the Temple, and carried the people into captivity—the good ones along with the bad. As God had explained, wickedness had gotten out of hand. They needed the time out to regain their sense of direction. Then after 70 years, just as other prophets had predicted, the Persians allowed the Israelites to go home. Another hundred years passed. While Governor Nehemiah was out of Jerusalem, the priests and the people again got themselves in thick with the pagans.

"Wasn't this exactly King Solomon's problem!" Nehemiah yelled when he came back. "He married unbelieving wives. They led him away from our God." A well-placed kick sent one culprit reeling. He punched another. "How can you do this?" His hand lashed out and grabbed away a fistful of hair from a third. "Never!" More hair. More punches. "Do you hear me!" More kicks. "Never!" More hair. "Never do this again!"

Nehemiah's attack had a startling effect, and his angry outbursts had results. The people began to distance themselves from their pagan neighbors and from their gods. They safeguarded the Temple. And kept the Sabbath.

Time passed.

They added rule to rule.

"We can't ever let ourselves do things like that again," they promised each other. "We must keep ourselves pure." They worked hard to show God they could obey Him by following all His rules. And they waited to receive the Messiah whom He would send to save them from their enemies.

More time passed.

"Show us a sign!" they demanded shortly after the turn of the millennium when a radical named Jesus began swaying the minds of the people. "A sign from heaven!"

The Man met them with a steady gaze. "You'll have no sign," He replied evenly. "No sign. Except for the sign of the prophet Jonah."

"Of Jonah?" someone mumbled. "What's to be learned from him?"

CHAPTER 11

GOD WORKS ON HEARTS

God! Jonah shifted, easing the weight off his left hip. *Ohhhh . . . God! Let me out of here!* His thoughts screamed with terror, but he dared not turn his feelings into real words, dared not express his loathing, his fear, of his claustrophobic tomb, dared not verbalize his dread of the rank, stifling closeness. Dared not vent his rage toward the God who had prepared this impossible phenomenon to pluck him from imminent death and . . .

"Ohhhh!"

His mind grasped thoughts of sunshine and blue skies and birds wheeling on the breezes, fresh breezes he could almost feel, and he imagined his lungs expanding with the freshness of morning air. But there was nothing but blackness! "Am I to be punished forever?" His body wrenched with a scream that broke from his throat. "Will I be engulfed eternally in this hell of hells?" His muscles tense, his nerves taut, he could feel his skin crawling. "God?" The roof of his mouth felt dry, his tongue heavy. "God! Help!"

The blackness smothered him. "Help!" The word was nothing more than a breath, yet the muscles in his upper back began to relax. "You hurled me here! Into the waves and the currents! I'm, sinking! God? Will You lift me up? Will You?" His words began to flow with poetic hope as he sensed a warmth, a strange, soothing warmth centering over the area of his heart. No. It was more of a presence—a calm, serene, soothing presence. "You will!" His writhing quieted. "You will bring my life up from the depths. You will! In Your holy temple You have heard me."

Suddenly he became bold with hope, with assurance, with belief that God had heard, that God would bring him back, that God would deliver him again into the land of the living. And his words now flowed with a pulsing, rhythmic ease. Long ago in his boyish dreams of the future, Jonah had placed his mighty men, stalwarts of God and country, as models for his ambitions. They carried sword and spear and conquered vicious foes. Yet in his dreams he carried neither sword nor spear. He held a pen. And with his pen he set words on parchment. Strong, lyrical words in parallelisms that would inspire thinking, that would change minds. As a child he had dreamed of producing poetic words that would rival the great psalms of centuries past.

"Beautiful." He relaxed in the warmth of the presence. Encouraged by his own prayer, his mind settled peacefully for the first time since the storm had overtaken the boat. "I've made up a prayer psalm. A psalm like one of David's." David, the great poet-king, had always been his hero of heroes. David—the man after God's own heart.

"After God's own heart?" Jonah half-raised onto an elbow. "The great David? The father of Uriah's wife's child?" He'd always carefully forgotten that part, left it with other matters he'd rather not think about. Slowly he slid back into position, knees tucked upward and under his crossed arms. The comforting presence still warmed the area of his heart, but he sensed a curiosity, a bewilderment.

David. The great David. And Bathsheba, only wife of Uriah the Hittite, one of the bravest and most daring of all the king's officers.

When David received Bathsheba's message that she was carrying his child, he did the only reasonable thing—he called Uriah to Jerusalem and urged him to go home to his wife. Make the soldier think he had fathered the child. Uriah's refusal cornered David.

Desperate, he felt forced into taking measures that were disgusting to even the worst of pagan kings. He wrote orders, then sealed his letter and placed it in the loyal Uriah's very own hand. "Take this to Joab, the commander," he said.

"Did David actually think that no one would ever suspect his part in Uriah's death? that no one would know he'd ordered his commander to set up Uriah in battle as an impossible-to-miss target?" Despite himself, Jonah's chuckle had a perverse edge to it. "Maybe Uriah didn't know, but God used a prophet."

A prophet! A dull heaviness pushed against the comforting warmth. *Nathan. A prophet. Sent by God.*

Nathan went to David and told him a story. A wealthy sheep rancher, he said, had stolen, then killed and roasted a poor man's only lamb—his pet, his only living companion—because he was too stingy to use an animal of his own to serve an unexpected visitor.

"Death to the one who would do such a thing!" David raged.

"You!" Nathan pointed straight at David. "You are the man."

"I . . ."

David's mouth dropped.

"I." Then . . . "I've sinned! Against the Lord!"

"The Lord has forgiven you, but . . ."

Nathan related the message God had sent. The baby would die because David's treachery against Uriah had disgraced God, had made Him a laughingstock to the surrounding nations. The baby did die, just as Nathan predicted, and the story, all of it, was in the scrolls. David's sin was made public to the entire world.

For some reason thoughts of Pharaoh and the plagues swirled back into Jonah's mind. Thoughts of how when the air and the ground and the palace seethed with flies, the king had called for Moses. "Go ahead. Take your people," he whined. "But not too far now, mind. And hurry. Get your God to do something about these flies."

"I will," Moses agreed. "Only don't you change your mind again."

"Of course not. Now go!"

Moses went. But as soon as the flies disappeared, so did the great pharaoh's promise.

"Brick-hearted brute." Jonah felt anything but generosity for the Egyptian king. "Got what he deserved. But David?" The contrast between the two stood stark. And yet . . . "After such a despicable act God could call David a man after His own heart?" Jonah's reasoning flowed more smoothly now. *God works on hearts, sends His Spirit, His prophets. The one heart hardens—like brick, like Pharaoh's. The other heart softens—like wax* . . . "Create a pure heart in me" (Ps. 51:10, TEV). That's what David had written after he had realized the grossness of his sin against Uriah.

The warm presence returned, strengthened. Suddenly Jonah realized that David's punishment had not cleared away his guilt, nor had it atoned for his sin. The death of the child did not make David right before God. David was made right before God because of his repentance, because he recognized what he had done and had pleaded for change within himself. Pharaoh, on the other hand, had turned the other way.

"Jonah."

The voice in the prophet's own heart spoke very quietly.

"I asked Moses to go. Moses was afraid. Yet he went.

"I asked Nathan to go. He went.

"I asked you . . ."

"Then Jonah prayed to the Lord his God from the belly of the fish."

—Jonah 2:1

JONAH'S PRAYER

"I called to the Lord out of my distress, and he
answered me; out of the belly of Sheol I cried, and you
heard my voice.

"You cast me into the deep, into the heart of the seas, and the flood surrounded me; all your waves and your billows passed over me.

"Then I said, 'I am driven away from your sight; how shall I look again upon your holy temple?'

"The waters closed in over me; the deep surrounded me; weeds were wrapped around my head at the roots of the mountains.

"I went down to the land whose bars closed upon me forever; yet you brought up my life from the Pit, O Lord my God.

"As my life was ebbing away, I remembered the Lord; and my prayer came to you, into your holy temple.

"Those who worship vain idols forsake their true loyalty. But I with the voice of thanksgiving will sacrifice to you; what I have vowed I will pay.

"Deliverance belongs to the Lord!" (Jonah 2:2-9).

"Then the Lord spoke to the fish, and it spewed Jonah out upon the dry land."

—Jonah 2:10

CHAPTER 12

A SECOND CHANCE

The sodden heap stirred. Hands groped out and fingers dug into the damp sand.

"Where . . ."

The person—that's what it was—lifted his head and pushed himself onto hands and knees. A volley of spray hissed behind him. His head turned just in time to see an enormous grayish oblong shape disappear beneath the sea's surface. As he stared, a triangular steel-gray fluke cut the wake like a large, rubbery, misshapen rudder. Then it too disappeared, and a patch of foamy bubbles bobbed up to ride in its place on the restless, green-blue water. "Woowww! It's big!"

And he found himself staring in awe at an empty sea—empty except for the cresting waves, a few seabirds, and a patch of flotsam to the right.

"Well, Jonah." The man spoke to himself as if he were another person. "Well . . ." Instead of getting up, he settled onto the sand, drew his knees up, locked them in his arms, and continued to watch the restless waves. "God's ways are . . ."

He searched for a word great enough to fill in the blank, a word that could give adequate meaning to what he'd just been through. "Infinite. Inscrutable. Unfathomable. Beyond comprehension or understanding." The expressions all seemed too hollow, too distant, too small to reach around and tell about the strange something that stirred in his soul. But then the experience was still too new, too beyond belief, for he himself to understand. All he knew was that he'd tried to run away when God had called, and that God had sent the storm and then the fish. Obviously God had reason for doing all that He had done, had reason for saving him, had reason for using such a strange, unbelievable means for keeping him alive.

"Whatever it is . . ."

Jonah stared toward the horizon, eyes seeing the wide expanse and yet not seeing. In a way he felt cleansed, as if because of his miraculous encounter changes had occurred within his own person, as if he were no longer the same Jonah, no longer the same person the sailors had thrown from the boat.

"It's true." As he clasped and unclasped his hands, his eyes fixed on the vague distance. "I'm not the same Jonah. I can never be the same. Not after . . ." He thought of the presence he'd sensed, how it had comforted him, how he'd been impressed with ideas he'd never before thought of. How . . .

With an abrupt shake of his head he broke out of his pensiveness and shoved himself to his feet. Stretching his arms upward, high, toward the heavens, he drew a series of full, deep breaths. Inhaling yet again, he drew refreshing air slowly through his nostrils, siphoning it in until it filled every corner of his lungs. Then he deliberately exhaled, and the air was forced out through his teeth with a high-pitched whistle. He let his arms drop.

Fresh air. Sun. Before, they'd always just been there. Just a normal part of everyday life.

Wriggling his toes in the sand, he bent and scooped some of the warm, white grains into the curve of his palm and then straightened and stretched out his arm and let them drain between his fingers, let himself relish their soft even flow. Let himself soak in the warmth of the morning sun on his back. As he enjoyed the breeze that swept back his long, dark hair, he melded into the aliveness of the moment. Suddenly he threw up his arms as if he had shaken off whatever had been bothering him. It was as if he were young and exuberant, heady with the new life of spring. He tossed back his head and shouted toward the heavens, "It's good to be alive! And . . ."

Sheltered by the cove, hidden from any human eyes, he clenched his fists and shoved his arms upward as if reaching toward the sky. His was the stance of a conqueror, of one to whom unexpected victory had come.

"God, if You ask again, I'll go!"

JONAH AND THE REPORTER

Wow! He's doin' OK now, isn't he? But if I'd have been there on the beach, I'd sure have had some questions to ask him.

Like what?

Well, for starters, What happened?

I mean, exactly how did that fish swallow you?

Was it scary?

How did it feel—

slithery,

squirmy,

or like what?

Did you go unconscious?

Or did it happen too quickly for your memory

to register

any particular sensations?

When—at what moment—did you realize that you were

actually alive

and inside a fish

and not dead?

How did you first react to that realization?
And how did you breathe
   and move
   and keep from getting digested?
Did God really talk to you
   —about Nineveh, I mean—
   out loud
   with a voice you could hear?
By the way, exactly what kind of fish was it?
Was it really a tiger shark, as some say?
Good questions, huh?
People say I ask good questions.
Used to be a reporter, you know.

What do You mean?

What more important angle? The fish business caused Jonah to make up his mind to go to Nineveh, didn't it? He had three days with nothing to do but think. What do You mean that he still did not understand what You want of Your people?

CHAPTER 13

WHICH WAY?

Jonah's feet and legs wanted to run, to dance, to declare their freedom from the cramped stillness they'd endured. His mind, though, clung to the empty beach, pleading for him to stay, to avoid for as long as possible returning to the world of people. And he stood where he was, torn between conflicting desires.

"Well . . ." He aspirated the word as a sigh. Forcing himself to turn, he measured the hill rising up between him and the world on the other side. As he drew another long, slow breath, his shoulders sagged, suddenly bending his shadow into a slumped caricature of the victorious hero he'd been only minutes earlier. He stared at it, not understanding. One moment he'd been alight with thankfulness to God, the next it was as though a door had suddenly burst within his mind, spilling out hyperacrid passions—dark, spiteful, and bitter—and forcing a dull-hot flush across his face, down his neck, and across his shoulders. A strange, trembling sensation tingled through his body, but he fought it, tried to shove it away, tried to calm himself. Tilting his head back, he started to open his mouth. Through puckered, dry lips he forced himself to speak. "I will go." A ridge of muscle tightened along his jaw. "I promised. And when . . ." His teeth clamped together, and he ground them back and forth, bottom teeth raking against the uneven surfaces of the top. Unconsciously he made a fist with his right hand and smacked it against the other, digging his knuckles in and twisting them back and forth against his palm, hard.

With white-knuckled self-discipline we can sternly force ourselves to go against our emotions and inclinations. We can push down resentments, contain angry feelings. Yet our depiction of Jonah's seesawing emotions reflects the plight many Christians encounter. On the peak of enthusiasm, wanting to do something great for God, they suddenly tumble headfirst into depression. Or, piqued by some trivial incident, they explode into a passion of rage.

Charles's musical talents had long made him a favored music director in his church. A younger man moved into the area and joined his church and choir. As time passed, the younger man began encouraging Charles to include more modern arrangements in their programs. "They don't fit our style of singing," Charles hedged. Others in the choir began asking for some of the same songs. "He's trying to take over," Charles complained to himself. His resentment grew. Then one day when Charles stopped by the pastor's office, he saw a sheet of music on the desk. "What's that?" he demanded.

"Just something your friend . . ." the pastor mentioned the young man's name.

"Friend!" Charles yelled. Suddenly a string of explicit four-letter word pictures began pouring from his mouth.

Unless resolved, repressed anger will surface. It may explode into a hot-tempered tirade, such as Charles was shocked to hear himself shouting. In extreme cases it may crack with cold, unreasoning fury, leaving us to stare at headlines screaming the horror of a lone gunman cutting down innocent children and then turning the gun on himself. More commonly, though, the feelings more or less hide under the surface, bobbing up now and again in sarcasm, gossip, criticism, tense mannerisms, irritated tones of voice, and the like.

"Christians shouldn't get angry like that," Charles later confided to his pastor. "I don't understand what happened."

Fortunately, the pastor had some training in dealing with anger, and he took the opportunity to counsel with Charles.

Feeling that anger is wrong, many Christians habitually repress their feelings in an effort to appear kind and gentle. Some become overnice people pleasers. Others turn into hard-on-themselves perfectionists. Both tendencies can be symptomatic of repressed anger. Other indicators of repressed anger can include excessive tiredness, the inclination to overwork, anxiety, a harsh and critical attitude, gossiping, and food or substance abuse. Contrary to what many people believe, repressing anger is not the same as turning the other cheek. By using misguided self-discipline, we can physically turn our faces to receive a blow on the other side. But that is not what Christ meant. Only when we have His spirit of forgiveness can we truly turn that other cheek.

If while in the fish, as supposed in the previous chapters, Jonah did reflect on lessons from the biblical scrolls, they had no obvious and immediate aftereffect. This is normal. Habits run deep. We may want to have Christ's spirit of forgiveness, may want to turn the other cheek when affronted, but as Charles discovered about himself, we do not know how. And like him we keep working at controlling our feelings. He had no idea of the power of his building resentment. "Shouting such terrible things? At the pastor yet?" He couldn't believe what he'd done. Few people can when trapped in similar circumstances.

Anger is one of the most powerful emotional forces. It is so powerful that the simple making of an angry face stimulates physiological responses even when one has no angry feelings. This happens to actors. If assigned to assume an angry appearance and to hold it long enough, an actor actually begins to have angry feelings. This being the case, imagine the powerful physiological impact of repressing anger. Good behavior, generous actions, and stern self-discipline may mask the anger, but all that goodness will never neutralize the unacknowledged and unresolved feelings. It will never generate a spirit of forgiveness or heal us. Until we deal with repressed anger and root out its basic cause, it will continue its poisoning influence, and as with the prophet Jonah, it will warp our concept of what God wants of us.

Back on the beach, a gigantic hissing startled the prophet. He turned abruptly and saw an enormous foaming crest curling into itself, flattening, pushing a froth-flecked layer of gray water onto the beach. Just then, beyond the breakers, a large, dark triangle momentarily rode on a gray-flanked swell. "No!" Jonah exclaimed, searching the area with his eyes, wanting them to trace out the reality. But he saw nothing more. Nothing out of the ordinary. "Was it?" he demanded of himself. "Was it my fish?"

In answer, he heard only the slap and sloshing as waves kept breaking in uneven, slow-motion sequence. One after the other they washed onto shore, then drained back and vanished into the restless sea. Like the waves, his churning emotions had broken and had rolled back into the normal restlessness of his mind.

"God has saved you." He spoke to himself as though reminding another person of a duty he was bound to perform. "Like Moses and Samuel, you must obey." Slowly he repeated the old and familiar advice that religious teachers had always given, forgetting already any newer ideas that may have come to him in the fish. Drawing another long breath, he said, "Well, can't stay here for always." Turning again, he forced deliberate steps toward the easiest slope of the hill. At the hill's crest he paused and in the distance saw two men working in a field. He headed toward them. After the proper exchange of pleasantries, he asked directions.

"On your way to Jerusalem, you say?" the older of the two asked.

Jonah nodded. "Which way?" he asked again.

"Stranger in these parts, are you?"

A quick nod.

"Where you coming from?"

"There." Jonah waved his hand toward the hill he'd just

climbed. "From the . . ." He started to say sea, then thought better of it. "Uh . . . that direction."

"The sea's just over that hill."

Another nod.

"Not anything else over there. No road. No path." The men seemed to be studying him as though they had other questions they wished to ask. Finally the younger did ask, "Are you all right, mister?"

"Sure, I'm fine. I was just . . ." *Just vomited onto the beach by a fish. Is that what I tell them?* "Well, I've been traveling quite some ways and stopped over there for a rest. Now, just point me toward the road to Jerusalem."

"Thataway." Both motioned toward a path forking toward the south. "Sure you're OK?"

Again Jonah nodded. *OK? Of course I'm OK.*

"That path'll take you to the road. Can't miss it."

"Thanks." Jonah started to turn. "Oh, by the way. What day is it?"

"Day?"

"Yeah."

"Are you sure you're all right?"

"Me?" Jonah forced a laugh. "Never felt better in my life." And with a quick wave and wishing the two a day of profitable labor and a future bountiful harvest, he turned toward the south. "And now I'll prove my thankfulness," he said to himself, squaring his shoulders. "I'll offer the sacrifices I've promised."

JONAH AND SACRIFICES

You're saying that it really didn't matter to You
whether or not he went to Jerusalem then? But it couldn't
have been that far. It's only 30 or so miles from Joppa. If . . .
Pardon? You wanted something else? You wanted

more than his sacrifices and thank offerings? You wanted more than for him to say that he would go if You asked again? You're saying that You were trying to tell him what You've always said? That what You did was another way of saying to him, "Rend your heart, and not your garments"? (Joel 2:13, NKJV)? That's what I still don't understand—that part about the heart.

CHAPTER 14

THE CALL

The tree stood proud in its tinsel and lights, a log burned in the fireplace, and the kitchen blended aromas of cookies, hot apple cider, and mandarin oranges. Our kids had just come in from a private shopping tour, whispering, wearing broad smiles, and carrying mysteriously bulky parcels. For me, all of that added to a special this-is-how-it-should-be, cozy-good Christmas feeling. As a youngster I'd dreamed of going places and of getting away from the loneliness of my childhood. Our move to British Columbia's beautiful, lake-filled Okanagan Valley, Canada's renowned four-season vacationland, had taken me as far as I wanted to go.

We had arrived.

I was convinced that we were in the right place doing the right thing. In a few years the kids would finish their own schooling and I could *retire* from teaching and devote full time to my first love, writing. The future looked rosy, the past had disappeared into the good humor of the season. Friends, family, and festivities filled the room. I still believed—and taught—our old Jonah bedtime story formula: pray, give yourself to your work, try to be good, and God will bless.

I prayed.

I worked.

I tried.

And I worried.

Some undefinable something was wrong.

It was as though God expected something more of me.

Then the telephone rang.

"What's the idea?" It was good friend Tami, long-distance from southern California.

"What idea?" I asked. "It's nearly Christmas. Merry Christmas!"

"Forget Christmas!" she snapped. "What's the meaning of these forms I got?"

"Forms? What forms? I didn't send you any forms."

"Not you. Church headquarters."

I could see no connection between forms from them and us, and I told her so.

"They're references. Something about you wanting to be missionaries."

"Ohhhhh . . . those." I laughed. "Pure formality. We *don't* want to be missionaries."

"Do you want me to fill them out?"

"Sure. Go ahead."

"You're not planning to be missionaries?"

"Of course not!"

"Then why these forms?"

I drew an exaggerated breath and then tried to explain that years earlier someone had suggested us as possible overseas mission candidates and that notes had come recently saying the office in charge of recruiting missionaries was updating files and would we please supply current information, that we were under no obligation . . . "Pure formality," I repeated. "Filled them out just to stop all their nagging. Made it plain we don't want to go. Not now. And . . . well, you didn't expect me to leave you off the list for references, did you?"

"Just don't leave me here and go off somewhere on the other side of the world."

"No worry." I laughed as if the very notion were unimaginable. "We're comfortable here. They've called twice before. Because we were needed here, we didn't go then. We have no intentions of going anywhere now. Maybe someday in the far-off future." I put down the receiver, supposing the matter was settled. Then on a January morning, scant weeks later, Date slipped into my classroom. "I just had a phone call," he whispered.

Since when did he interrupt my classes to tell me about his phone calls? (He was principal of a Christian school in which I taught English.)

"From headquarters."

So? They call frequently.

"There's a call coming."

Call and telephone go together, right?

"There's a school in Africa."

Call. School. Africa. I grabbed his arm and turned toward the door. "Kids'll be fine," I whispered back, finally putting words to tongue. "I just gave an in-class assignment." Then in the hall: "What kind of call to where in Africa?"

"Director of a mission school in Rwanda."

"Rwanda?" That was long before the 1994 tropical holocaust that made the little African country stand out like a sore thumb on the world map. "Where's that?"

He shrugged.

"Let's go to the library."

Between the covers of an encyclopedia we found descriptions of the tiny equatorial country perched on Africa's continental divide. Land of bananas, papayas, and volcanoes, French-speaking . . .

"French-speaking!"

Because of Date's degree in French, the easy no slipped away. Joann attended the local college, and Jon had nearly finished secondary school. We had our home, a sailboat down at the yacht club, and work contracts signed. Security. Against that I visualized

78

a genial, ready-to-listen mission school administrator. Date easily fit that picture. But the smiling-lady stereotype—enthusiastic, face alight, recounting stories to a mass of eager-eyed children—now, that was something else.

"Me?"

"You? A missionary?" I understood the surprised voice. "But you said . . ." It was Tami again.

"Plans change."

"You are really going to Africa?"

"Yes."

Silence hummed on the line for a long moment. Then: "I can't picture you being a missionary."

When I finally replied, my words were a quiet "I can't either."

"Then why . . ."

"Because . . ."

How do you explain, even to a best friend, about the uneasiness within your own soul, about hidden-away resentments pushing you to get away, about the vague notion suggesting that giving yourself as a missionary might make everything right between you and God?

"Well," I finally managed, "it's not quite halfway around the world."

"Do you really want to go?"

"Look. There's a phone only 12 miles from the mission."

"Twelve miles!"

"They say it's less than an hour's drive."

"Like I said, do you really want to go? Do you really want to be a missionary?"

Silence again. Finally, "I'm not sure I even know what a missionary is."

We packed, sold our home, settled the kids in college, and left. During mission orientation classes an instructor talked about cross-cultural communication and about bringing change to others,

"But," she continued, "you'll find that the biggest change you experience will be what happens to you."

That sounded perfect. I left for Africa sure that we were doing the right thing.

JONAH AND ME?

Jonah?

And me?

Like I said, no connection. You called—we went.

Jonah had a problem with obedience. When You called him, he ran. And he tumbled into one hard lesson. And boy, did that change him!

Huh?

I still need to look deeper?

Into my heart?

For what?

THE SECOND CALL

J onah stirred. Was that a voice? A cold prickling tingled down his back, and a dull heaviness snapped around his chest and stomach. He wanted to run. Or better yet, to push himself under his cloak and curl into a small, unrecognizable huddle.

"Jonah!"

It was a voice—*the* voice. He forced himself upright. "Yes?"

"Go to Nineveh!"

"Uhhh . . ."

"Proclaim the message."

The raw suddenness of the order grated along his conscience. *I don't want to. I don't. I . . .* But he didn't voice what he was feeling, didn't dare, and his throat muscles clenched together until they banded around his neck like tight, searing shackles. Finally he forced himself to form the promise that in his heart of hearts he had hoped he would never have to put into practice. "Yes, Lord." His voice was dull and flat. "I'll go."

Numbly he went through his preparations, headed through the door and down the street, forcing one foot in front of the other. How he wished he were not Jonah, not this Jonah, not the Jonah with a message, not the Jonah of the fish. His thoughts turned like an ungreased wheel. Of all people, he should know what God did to those who did not obey.

Unconsciously he flared his lips and drew in air until it whistled between his teeth, until he could feel it stinging against his gums. His hand tightened around his walking staff, clamping it until his fingers must press their prints into the wood. "I'm going!" He pounded his staff against the packed earth as if defying anyone to suggest the contrary. "And I'll preach." His lips flared out explosively. "And they'll find what it's like to meet a real God. Humph! Thinking their imitation gods can save them. Their idols. Humph! Gross inventions! Perverted like they are!"

Propelled by his impassioned thoughts, Jonah swung into long, brisk strides. "They'll hear preaching like they've never heard before, they'll hear doom and double doom, they'll quake in their very sandals. Every one of them will know the voice of God has spoken."

Suddenly, without any good reason, he was seeing himself as a boy. Skinny, too short for his age, shoulder blades sharp under the cloth they'd tossed off to him for a shirt, he stood head down, arms braced to ward away blows. And in front of him, his father's brother, shouting as only he could shout, the air blistering with his angry, scathing damnations. "What's the matter with you, letting the . . ."

In his mind Jonah had always fought away his uncle's bullying tirades, but in real life he had dared not speak a word in his own defense, dared not open his mouth.

"You'll never learn! Never! Never! Never! You'll never amount to a thing!"

"Will to." Jonah startled himself by suddenly shouting aloud. "You'll see. Everyone'll see." Stopping abruptly, he swung around to check if anyone was near enough to hear. No one. Then he spun about again, his mantle swinging into a swirl of color, and strode on.

Whether or not such boyhood scenes actually took place to contribute to Jonah's attitude, his behavior marked a very immature person. Abuses suffered during the growing years do stunt emotional growth. Children are also affected by unresolved abuses handed down to them from parents and grandparents. Generations of Israelites had suffered Assyrian violations. Whether because of this, or personal abuse, or for other reasons, Jonah carried an obvious chip on his shoulder. He had never learned to deal with it. Many authorities agree that unless taught skills for resolving their anger and resentment for what has happened, most abused children will grow up incapable of dealing with anger on an adult level. When anger strikes, they tend to act and react with the maturity of the age level at which during childhood life deeply hurt them. It makes no difference whether they were rejected, or whether they were physically, emotionally, or sexually violated. The results are the same. Maturation is *frozen* at that point, and the hurting children grow into adults with only kid skills in coping. I remember a certain incident that illustrates the pattern.

"You had no right!" Rigid Shoulders faced me, standing in midroad.

I felt my face stiffen.

"You . . ."

Her words whirled hard, punching with accusation. Inside, I fought the charges one by one. "But . . ." My throat quivered around a justifying retort.

"No!" Her answer slammed back, cutting me off. "You . . ."

One after the other, Rigid's complaints sizzled toward me. Then she turned and stalked off.

"Christian?" In my mind I pictured my arms grabbing out like . . . well, like they had on a long-ago spring day. It was one of those warm, invigorating days after a wet and stormy winter, and life was coming back into its full. School was out for the day. I dawdled. The other third graders had gone. The teachers were nowhere in sight. Then I heard the kid coming. *The kid!*

In my mind, he epitomized all the meanness I had endured day after day from him and his friends. Their taunting. Their repulsive commentaries regarding my larger-than-normal proportions. Their refusal to include me in their games. I'd had enough!

His hateful, high-pitched voice sang through the hall.

Stepping back out of sight, I planted myself solidly. Just as he burst through the doorway, I grabbed out. "You'll pay!" I screamed.

His flannel shirt filled my hands.

I swung.

His feet jerked up.

I put all my weight into the swing.

His shirt tore from my grip.

My feet hardened in place like wooden blocks.

My eyes followed the deliberate arc of his blimplike body . . .

Soaring . . .

Across the cloakroom . . .

Crash!

He broadsided the janitor's mop bucket.

Water flew.

He yelled.

I ran.

No one ever mentioned the spilled water.

Not even *the kid*. In fact, he never uttered another word in my direction—either good or bad.

And now I stood in the road glaring after the woman's shoulders. "Christian?" Of course, I would never ever dare actually reach out and grab her by the shoulders and throw her, but . . . The idea of her soaring above the hedge, beautifully splay-armed and out of control, crashing down onto her well-trimmed and heavily thorned tea roses. If I had not been so angry, I could have laughed. I wanted her to hurt, to have the justice she deserved like . . . like what? Like the spanking I'd wished for Cousin Freddy back when he had broken my toy dog. My fingers curled, clawing against my palms.

"Vengeance is Mine" (see Rom. 12:19; Lev. 19:18). The text flashed into my mind. Taking a deep breath, I gritted my teeth. After all, I was an adult—an adult Christian. It was not my place to fight back, but God's. He would . . .

What would He do? Give her a divine spanking when my mother had refused to spank Cousin Freddy? "But she did it on purpose!" I wanted to yell, as if my complaints could persuade God to take the action I wanted. "She did! She did it on purpose!"

Most adults see others as acting toward them intentionally, with maliciously thought-out motives. "They did it on purpose." On the other hand, we defend our own actions. "I had no choice. I was forced into it. I did it because . . ." Our becauses handily excuse behavior that we would find inexcusable in others.

"It's not that I actually want anything bad to happen to her." That's what I said later when my injured feelings settled enough for me to think through the matter. "It's the principle." As far as I was concerned, anyone with an ounce of sense could see that she was clearly in the wrong and that I was clearly in the right. "I want her to be put in her place. I want her to right what she's done. To stop accusing me. To . . ." As surely as Jonah wanted to have his prophetic reputation vindicated by God's vengeance on the Ninevites, I wanted to have my name cleared.

"Vengeance is Mine," God says. "I will repay." He makes His position clear in the song Moses wrote down for the Israelites. The Lord will punish His enemies. And He will have mercy on those who serve Him (see Deut. 31; 32).

Leaving our enemies in God's hands, though, as Jonah's story will show, does not necessarily settle matters the way we want. I knew that God's mercy and grace are available to everyone. That's what the Bible says. If I left Rigid Shoulders in His hands, and if His Spirit worked on her heart, and if she would pay attention, then she would . . .

I stopped, startled by where my thoughts were leading me. She would be changed, not punished.

We humans thrive on punishing others. God thrives on re-deeming us. While we want to make others hurt for what they've done, God longs to heal us from what we've done. Although we insist that others change their attitudes, God offers us a change of heart. We try to force others to do things our way, but God invites us to choose to live His way. And when we want to be what we want to be, He wants us to be like Him.

Jonah's fish experience helped to change his attitude—at least enough to make him go to Nineveh—but he still held feelings of spite and vengeance, and he wanted the Ninevites to *burn*.

CHAPTER 16

A LESSON LEARNED?

W ell! Well! Well! If it isn't Jonah!"

Jonah's head jerked up. "Enos?"

"Well! Well! Well!" the tall man boomed out again. "Our very own Jo-o-nah. Our prophet." He reached out both arms to pull his townsman into an embrace. "It's been a long time." Letting his arms drop, he stepped back.

Jonah dipped his head and his head covering flounced forward, momentarily screening his face.

"The last I heard of you . . ." Enos shook his head. "I was in Joppa not so long after you sailed—business, you know. Hmh-hmh-hmh!" The deep-down, forced chuckle caused Jonah to arch an eyebrow. "Was still there when your ship came back. Is it true?" The man paused. "Nice mantle, that," he interjected abruptly, gesturing toward the red, brown, and white stripped outer robe Jonah wore. Then he repeated himself, emphasizing each word. "Is it true? I mean, those incredible stories the sailors told about there being a storm and all? Were you really running away from God? I mean, really, were you thinking you could escape Him?" Enos tipped back his head and forced out another low-bass "Ha-Ha-Ha!" Then without pausing, he rushed on. "Is it true about the fish? Did a fish really swallow you? But I see you here as good as always. What happened?"

A kind of half-smile began to curve across Jonah's face. "Well . . ."

Something about Enos's candidness brought back the bravery Jonah had sensed on board the ship. And now he really did smile. "Well . . ." *How do you put what happened into words?* "God did send a fish. It brought me back. And . . ." Jonah took another step forward. "Now, if you'll excuse me, I'm on my way to find a caravan to Nineveh."

"Well, I never!" Enos took a surprised step to the side of the path.

Jonah hurried by. "Stay well," he called back over his shoulder. "I have a message to deliver."

The other man stared after him in surprised, though mistaken, admiration.

Jonah strode on.

He would obey.

The prophet would preach.

By fulfilling his duty as God's chosen messenger, he would prove that he had learned his lesson.

Looking in on Jonah through the sparse details of the Bible story, we wonder how he could be so blindly self-centered and how God could be so patient. After undergoing God's corrective discipline in the storm and fish experience, Jonah did change his outward direction. He had neither hardened his heart, as had Pharaoh, nor pleaded for a new heart, as had David. Instead he had simply decided to comply with the directive. His anger still smoldered, and we see him acting as if he had no idea that the scrolls proclaimed: "Love the Lord your God with all your heart, with all your soul, and with all your strength" (Deut. 6:5, TEV). "Do not take revenge on anyone or continue to hate him, but love your neighbor as you love yourself" (Lev. 19:18, TEV).

In his prayer from inside the fish, Jonah had sneered at the Ninevites' worship, calling it worthless (Jonah 2:8). At the same time he promised sacrifices in thankfulness for his salvation. He seemed determined to worship and obey God carefully, and in return he wanted the Ninevites dead. After all, God's message for Nineveh was clear. In 40 days God would destroy the city. But would God stick to His guns? To keep his dignity, a prophet needs a God who follows through with His promises. Many Christians, in their anger, still want their dignity upheld by a vengeful God avenging their hurts. "If You are a God of love and justice, then do something!" they cry out, imagining that His revenge will magnify their own cruel wishes.

God works through life's tough experiences to reach our hearts, but not even He can make us see the ungodliness of our inner selves if we do not pay attention to Him. Neither can He force us to change unless we choose to be transformed. He has given us liberty, has endowed us with the power of choice. God can send prophets, work miracles, and intervene through others on our behalf. The Lord can send His Spirit. But He cannot forcefully alter our attitudes or inner persons. We will never change or be changed unless we ourselves first become convinced that we have a problem that needs correcting. Even then we have to choose change. That transformation includes the way we respond to and deal with our feelings of anger. Until we understand and accept that we have a problem, we will repulse any message suggesting that we need to change.

Many years ago I received a letter containing a direct message. I stood clutching it, my hand trembling. It was signed, "A concerned friend." A hot stinging sensation rose upward along the veins of my neck. "But who? Who would write this? To . . . to me?" I picked up the envelope. Turned it over.

No name.

No return address.

The postmark gave no clue.

I looked toward the window. It could be anyone. Any one of scores of people. "Is that . . . is that what they think? That I . . . that I need to understand God's love?" Suddenly I felt that nameless person staring in at me. Staring in at my private life. "Well!"

With a few quick motions, the paper—and its message—became nothing more than a handful of tattered shreds.

Many years later I attended a gathering of former classmates. "Do I know you?" The questioning face, not the first of the evening, turned toward me. "Were you in our class?"

"Yes. I'm . . ." *After 30-some years everyone else still looks . . . well, somewhat the same.*

"Of course, you remember her!" someone said. "She's . . ."

"No! I'd never have guessed!"

"I left soon after graduation."

"You've changed."

"Pictures?"

I nodded, pulling a photo album out of my purse.

"Your daughter's really beautiful."

Smiles.

"And your son. Fine-looking. What'd you say he does?"

"Research. Math."

"Your husband! Good looking too, isn't he?"

Another nod. *Of course. I always wanted the best.*

Then quietly, meeting my eyes, my long-ago classmate asked, "What happened?"

Pause. A little maturity. A little professionalism. And . . . *How do you put into easy words so they'll understand about second chances and opportunities and discovering the need for change . . . and about . . . well . . . about God working a lot on a backward heart?*

Good things can happen in anyone's life, but much depends upon attitude and choices made. But that's getting ahead of my story. And Jonah's.

JONAH AND CHANGE

"So Jonah set out and went to Nineveh, according to the word of the Lord."

—Jonah 3:3

You mean that after the fish Jonah considered himself a changed person? That he thought that he had done enough? Even with all his angry feelings? Boy, he sure needed to take a good look at himself. To see how he felt about the Ninevites. Godlike? Huh! Talk about selfish! As a prophet he was self-centered to the core. He certainly needed to learn a thing or two.

What are You saying? That he's not the only one? I'm not sure that I get what You mean.

CHAPTER 17

SHAME!

The heavy walls fronting the mighty Tigris River stretched far into the distance. "B-i-i-i-g!" The word aspirated with pure amazement. Jonah tried to deal with the impact of what he was seeing. By comparison, the walled seven or eight hectares of Samaria, the capital city of King Jeroboam II, were a mere nothing. "Bigger even than Jerusalem!" He tried to make sense of the grandeur and obvious prosperity of the sprawling pagan metropolis. "Inconceivable!"

When he finally slipped through the portals of Nineveh's grand gate, pocketed away among a colorful bevy of merchants, with their wares, and a scattering of citizens, Jonah felt awed and insignificant at the same time. The gate's massive arches, the enormous supporting towers, the wide boulevard leading toward the center of the city, the lavish houses fronting it. He let himself be swept along with the crowd, not minding where he went, not noticing the unevenness of the stones beneath his feet, not feeling the sun's burning heat. Ahead an immense platform supported a massive, many-columned building.

"A temple?" He stopped, feet set wide apart, his hands tucked into his belt. "To the goddess Ishtar?" Hoofbeats clattered in the distance. "To that savage, immoral icon of pagan vulgarity?" He continued to stare, oblivious to the others scurrying away from where he stood. "Incredible!"

The hoofbeats pounded closer, and with them came the ring of metal on stone. But his mind was busy. "Such magnificence!"

"Stand back!"

Jonah drew his shoulders up.

"Stand back!"

With a start Jonah realized that the voice was yelling at him, that he stood solid in the path of a chariot team. As he jumped, his right foot twisted under his weight, throwing him into a bouncing, backward stagger.

"Look!" a childish treble shrieked. "That funny man."

Like an upright, overweight pig struggling for balance, Jonah wobbled back another pace and a half. His stick flung out crazily, and the fringe of his robe flapped toward the flank of the near horse.

"Watch it!"

Jonah staggered to a halt, now bracing himself with his stick, his eyes freezing on the three helmeted forms in the chariot.

"Peasant!" The driver's voice thundered above the noisy hooves.

The prophet caught his balance and glared after the chariot's occupants. "Peasant, is it?" Adjusting his mantel, he grasped its blue fringes and held them out so everyone could see their excessive wideness, could see that he was a person not to be trifled with. He had ordered the border made exceptionally wide to show that he held faithful and privileged allegiance to the God of heaven.

"Look at him!" the same childish treble insisted, but the grown-ups ignored the pretentious figure and walked by as though the prophet were not there. Two headed one way, a few another, others stopped at booths near the temple, while still others made their way toward closed doors lining the street opposite. Throbbing, erotic sounds drifted in from a band of musicians playing somewhere around the corner.

"And they call that worship?" Jonah dropped his hands and moved toward the shade of an overhanging balcony. His thoughts circled back to Jerusalem. A different sort of anger welled up in

Jonah now. How could people worship human emotions instead of the true God? How could they give themselves to a goddess who encouraged immorality and lewdness in the name of spirituality? How could they be snared by the raucous music, the obscene dances? Yet even the brilliant King Solomon, led astray by his heathen wives, had fallen under the same spell and had even offered his own children as sacrifices—his very own children. "Bosheth!" The Hebrew exploded under his breath with the force of a four-letter word. "Shame," that's what it meant. "Bosheth!" His lips curled again, derisively twisting the word Ashtoreth, the Hebrew name for Ishtar.

Thoughts of his sacrifices contrasted sharply with what was happening around him. He'd bought the fattest and finest bull that money could buy. Following Moses' stipulations for paying vows, he'd presented it at the door of the Temple along with bread of every kind—fat loaves and thin, some baked with yeast, some without, cakes brushed with olive oil, cakes made with flour mixed with olive oil. "I offered the best!" He tossed his head back, and to the boy who was still watching him, he seemed to be looking down his nose toward a charm vendor sitting across the street. "Now, that was a real sacrifice," he told himself. "And the feast afterward . . ."

At the Temple the priest had taken his share of the meat and bread almost too eagerly, but when Jonah and his guests finally gathered at their table, he knew the Lord could not help being pleased. "I made good my promise."

With his eyes he again measured the massiveness of the structure fronting the grand boulevard. "Bosheth!" For him the word included every name by which the venerated daughter of heaven was known—Ashtoreth, Astarte, Ishtar, Venus. The wife of Baal. The goddess of love and fertility. The goddess of war. The goddess born from an egg two fishes carried to the seashore. "Grross!" A raised platform, empty except for a handful of meandering pigeons, caught his attention. He'd thought to begin his preaching the next day. *But why not now?* With a loud tapping of his staff, he shoved himself toward the high steps leading up to the platform.

Some passersby paused. "Is that man crazy?" The boy pointed toward Jonah's portly figure as the prophet hefted himself upward step by step. "Dunno," someone replied. "Strange, anyway."

Once atop the platform Jonah braced his feet wide and raised his staff. "Yet 40 days!" The words screamed through his throat.

More people stopped. Men dressed for leisure. A few soldiers, weapons bristling in the morning brightness. More children. And women, hair plaited, faces painted, arms wearing bracelets hung with the impossible-to-mistake sexual features of their goddess. The general posture reflected a people lost in the emotional high of a life dominated by music, sex, and alcohol.

"Nineveh will be destroyed!" he thundered directly toward three women. Obviously, they were devoted to the business of charming men into the specialized worship of their deity.

"Who is that guy, anyway?" The question passed back and forth through the crowd.

"He's crazy." The boy spoke loudly to his friends, who had come to stand with him.

"Yes!" Jonah pounded his staff, rattling the iron-hard wood against the stone. "In 40 days Nineveh will be destroyed!"

"Nineveh?" someone said. "Surely not this Nineveh!"

"This very Nineveh!" Jonah shook his staff in the direction of the cluster where his heckler stood. "That is the message of God!"

"And what god might that be?"

"The God of heaven."

"But right here we have the queen of heaven!"

Glaring at the one who dared suggest any comparison between the two, Jonah shot back his scathing rebuttal. "The God of heaven, before whom no one dare mouth disrespect. The great Yahweh. The all-powerful Creator. The . . ."

"Ha! Ha! Ha! Nineveh has stood since the days of the ancient

Nimrod (Gen. 10:8-12), the great hunter-king. And now you say your God . . ."

"See! Didn't I say he's crazy?" The boy was whispering now.

"Say! Isn't 'e the one?" With a quick thrust of his elbow, a husky, rough-clad fellow standing just ahead of the boy dug into the ribs of his companion.

Pointing toward the two, the boy motioned to his friends to listen.

"Well, I'll be!" The other man stared toward Jonah. "It's him, all right. The runaway. Sure's God's in 'is heaven, it's him right and proper."

"What's that you say?" A tall, dark-skinned man on the modest side of middle age gathered his robe and edged a careful step nearer the two.

"That preacher there." A muscled arm pointed in Jonah's direction. "Aboard our ship, 'e was, an' a storm came up, likes o' what we'd never seen."

"Wild!" The second gravelly voice exclaimed. "Like when the gods are very angry. Never 'spected to see land again." And he pounded the flat of his hand against his broad chest.

"Shoutin' at us ta cast lots, all the other sailors were. And we did, and it landed on this'un here." Again the arm swung in Jonah's direction.

"Forty days! And God will destroy Nineveh!" Jonah's piercing eyes fixed the two men. "Remember. You were there. You know I didn't want to come."

Both nodded. "If it'uz me, I'd lissen ta 'im," the first called out.

The boys looked at each other, eyes round.

"Yep. Lissen ta 'im. His God ain't no god o' foolin' 'round. Said 'is God tole 'im ta come here ta Nineveh ta preach. And what'd 'e done?"

"Ran away, 'e did," the other interjected. "Di'n't wanna come here, so 'e headed off fer Spain."

"Tole us ta throw 'im in the sea, tha's what 'e said. Throw 'im in the sea, and the storm'd stop." The first had taken back the story. "Di'n't want ta! Not us! Play games? Wi' the God o' hev'n?"

"But Cap'n made us. And . . ."

A look of unbelief spread over both faces as if they were seeing again what had happened on the boat.

"Wind stopped."

"Waves quieted down right then an' there, they did."

"And we saw a fish."

"Bigger than the biggest we'd ever seen. We're watchin' and we saw it swallow 'im. A fish!"

"Cap'n ordered sacrifices," the other said. "To his God." The words of the story came slower and more clearly now. "And all o' us—everyone workin' on that ship—vowed to worship the God o' heaven forever."

"Now look—'e's 'ere preachin'!"

"Nope. I'd pay attention, I would," the other added.

"Yet 40 days!" Jonah shouted again.

"Don't figure I'll be staying 'round here no 40 days."

"Me neither," echoed the second sailor. And both turned in the direction of the main gate.

The boys stared after them. "What should we do?"

"Dunno," the first said now.

"D'ya still think he's crazy?"

"I . . ."

"I'm going home!" A third spoke decisively. "This is getting too spooky."

"Let's go!" Several of the others spoke at once. As if on signal, they all turned and ran.

Jonah climbed down from the platform, not paying any attention to them or to the sailors or to the crowd in general. Dutifully he carried his message from one section of the city to another. He shouted from street corners, from platforms, from the steps of buildings. Once he stood under a war monument. He waved his hand toward the carvings. Captives with ears missing, captives with noses hacked off, victims with bodies carved up in scenes too gross to be put to tongue. "Nineveh will pay!" he ranted at his hearers.

As he crisscrossed quarter after quarter, stories of the strange events that had brought him to their city raced ahead of him. "If his God could send a fish . . ." By the third day the crowds were larger yet. Faces now ashen, they gathered about the strange preacher. "Repent" a voice cried out.

Others echoed the cry. "Repent!"

"Nineveh will be destroyed." With a flourish of his stick, Jonah shouted a final warning. Then he turned and retraced his steps toward the main gate. "This is it," he told himself. "This is the end of the wicked Nineveh."

And the prophet's words were about to be fulfilled in a way for which he was not prepared.

CHAPTER 18

DO SOMETHING!

J onah hunched forward on the stone ledge, chin cupped in his hand. Cornered against an abutment shielding him from the sun, he held a protected view of the main boulevard and market plaza. Instead of the usual crowds, he saw only pigeons. The birds picked among the stones, murmuring and crooning to themselves over an extraordinarily uninterrupted breakfast. A crooked smile played along Jonah's lips, and he could feel a trembling of excitement. He chuckled. The evening before, people had literally jumped away from his shadow as he passed, and now, except for the birds, the marketplace and the streets were empty. No vendors. No shoppers. No noisy chariot wheels. Nothing.

A distant clattering caught his ear. He straightened, at first thinking he heard someone shouting. Definite hoofbeats were nearing along a street. Then a horse cantered into view, rags draping its powerful shoulders. The rider, lean and muscular with a short, dark cloth knotted at his waist, reined in across from a row of houses beyond the market. With a flourish, he held up a clay tablet.

"By order of His Royal Highness, King Adad-nirari III." For years Adad-nirari III had ruled the Assyrian kingdom from his palace in Nineveh. (Centuries later historians would redesignate the years of his reign as 810 B.C. to 782 B.C.) Even Jonah had heard complaints about his weak, nonaggressive leadership. The prophet leaned forward now, straining to understand the words.

"From the moment of hearing this decree no man or woman or child is to eat anything." The courier's tones echoed along the street. "All persons, all cattle, and all sheep are forbidden to eat or to drink."

Clusters of people materialized and stood like mindless silhouettes along the edges of the buildings. Jonah had been near the palace when the king himself had come out and had made a great show of taking off his royal robes and of putting on a rough sack-shaped garment and settling himself onto a heap of ashes. *Ashes, yet!* Jonah thought, raising an eyebrow. *As if God will take notice.*

"All persons and all animals must wear sackcloth."

"Animals? Sackcloth?" Jonah eyed the restless horse, its forelegs shifting as if it were trying to ease away from the rough, prickly camel hair cloth draped over its shoulders.

"Everyone must pray earnestly to the God of heaven.

"Everyone must give up his or her wicked behavior.

"Everyone must give up his or her evil actions."

The man read the orders off as if they were items on a military checklist. The people met each one with silent nods. Just then a goat clattered toward the watering place, its mouth gaping a low, mournful "a-a-a-a." A dark rag straggled from a cord tied round its middle, slapping like a piece of loose skin against the animal's hindquarters. No one but Jonah noticed when it butted its head against an empty water jar. "A-a-a-a," it pleaded again.

The courier read on. "Perhaps God will change His mind."

"Hmmmph!" Jonah's disgusted snort was louder than he'd intended. "Them! Change the mind of God?"

"Perhaps He will stop being angry. Perhaps we will not die."

When he finished reading, the courier carefully slipped the clay tablet into a pouch. "Hear ye! Hear ye!" His hearers kept their silence. "This is the conclusion of the royal command of His Royal Highness, King Adad-nirari III." With that, he reined his horse around and pointed him in the direction of the palace stables.

Before long Jonah could see people settling themselves in front of their houses, sitting, heads down, dark pitiful humps under coarse cloths. Some tossed ashes and dust into the air, letting it settle over their heads and bodies. Several cows wandered in from who knew where. A straggling of goats and sheep followed, dark rags dangling about their backs. They nosed here, pushed there. The shuffling of their hooves blended with a dissonant wail that had begun to rise above every quarter like an unseen fog. Suddenly a sharp crescendo of songlike cries broke above the others. "God of heaven, hear our prayers! God! Hear us!"

"God!" Jonah abruptly pushed himself up and stared into the sky. "Are You listening to them?" He stamped the butt of his staff against the cobbles. "That charade? That pathetic pagan charade?" He stamped his staff down again and pivoted toward the gate. The sun poured down, and heat shimmered up from the naked stones. "Well?" Thumping his staff along in quick jabs, he slung his feet into hasty steps. "Show Your justice!" He grabbed at his mantel's thick edging with his free hand and crushed it into a hard knot. "That's what I said before I left home!" He drew a quick breath. "That's why I ran. Why I tried to go to Spain. I knew what You're like. I knew You'd do this. I knew!

"I knew! I knew!" Echoes of his own mutterings pounded back at him. Braking his headlong strides, he looked up. Mud bricks arched high above him. Digging a heel into the rutted and uneven surface beneath his feet, he spun around. In the distance, framed by the gate's tunnel-like entrance, the pillared temple, its domes sunbathed, its proud stone statue magnificently alive in mottled sunlight and shadow, stood silent. Before it, the boulevard disappeared under moody shadows cast by the now-empty porches. No singing. No laughing or shouting. No signs of the usual crowds of the partying shrine worshipers. No indolents lounging on the steps.

"Nineveh!" Jonah spat out the name.

101

As if in reply, the wails seemed to billow toward him, to pour as though funneled between the massive buildings. Growing. Swelling until they wrapped around him, pressing in, choking, throbbing against his ears.

"Stop it! Stop!"

If anything, the painful clamoring grew louder.

With a quick swipe he let go of his robe, threw his clenched staff upward, and shook it toward the mud-brick walls arching over him. "I knew it! I knew it!" He pounded the staff down now. Whirling around, he hurried toward the light flaring at the end of the gate passage. "Loving! Merciful!" His words jerked with the pounding of his feet. "Patient! I knew You'd change Your mind. That's what You're like!"

His staff beat a tatoo rhythm. "Too good. Too kind. Too forgiving." He threw his arm outward. "Won't punish!" His hand smacked against the wall. Startled, he brought his knuckles to his mouth, then rubbed them against the back of the hand that held his staff. Despite the smarting pain, he did not break stride. "I knew it!" He rubbed his smarting hand again. "God! Let me die. I'm better off dead than alive." He broke into the broad daylight of the open countryside.

"What right do you have to be angry?"

Abruptly Jonah stopped and tilted his head, as if expecting to hear the question again.

Silence. Except for the distant wailing.

He could just picture the welcome he'd get when he arrived back home in Israel. "Prophet?" Jeering voices. Pointing fingers. "Thought you said Nineveh was finished!" Swinging toward the east, he yelled "God" again and broke into long, stomping strides.

God remains the number one target of our anger. Like Jonah, we yell and accuse and blame Him when things go wrong. We also attack and blame others when they don't fit our expectations of what Christians should be. Years before our move overseas, the principal at another Christian school where I'd taught decided to raise campus standards. When he detailed his ideas, I felt the blood rise hot around my neck. "Some Christian educational environment!" I wanted to retort. But I held my tongue. Codes soon governed everything from hemlines to hairstyles. One of the girls, a gentle and sensitive person, had the knack for making herself look good.

"Too much makeup!" the principal decreed of her.

He sent her to the washroom with orders not to come out until she looked better. Time and again her mirror and his eyes could not agree on the meaning of *better*. His inflexibility inflamed her streak of stubbornness. Their wills locked.

I found her crying in the bathroom. "Why me?" She choked back sobs. "Why's he always picking on me? It's not fair!"

I went to the man.

"She has to go!" he yelled.

I talked about love and encouragement, but my words were clipped and hard, and they bounced off him like pebbles tossed against a solid stone wall.

He remained adamant.

I stormed off to the superintendent of schools.

The girl stayed, but no one alluded to the need of sackcloth and repentance for anyone, or of special needs, or of how our actions mirror our own concept of God.

"I hate your school!" the girl raged after graduation. "Christians? Nothing but mean! *Mean!* If that's what your God's like, He's . . ."

Though the principal seemed to me like an angry Jonah, yelling doom at her and being unwilling to meet her needs, her words hurt. Despite his do-it-my-way-or-else approach, other students managed his rules and even liked and supported the school; they attended church and had a growing relationship with God. I wondered what made the difference.

"Attitude," others said. "She has to learn respect."

The answer sounded simple, but I saw the unloving behavior of the principal and those who supported him as being responsible for her attitude. A school principal has to meet expectations of several groups—the school board, the parents, and the students themselves—and the man tried, by forced discipline, to encourage good Christian deportment. At the time, blinded to his good intentions, I saw only the sad results on the girl and on others who did not fit the mold. He wanted them to make good choices, but she, as I later realized, had sensed only rejection. She felt rejected by him, and by the school, the church, and even the God he represented.

As Christian teachers, parents, and adults, we do have the responsibility for helping young people learn to make good choices and of pointing them to a God who in His love has given us the power of choice. Instead, out of our own ignorance and pain, we pass on our misconceptions and faulty coping styles. "God is the answer," I told the girl, believing what I said, not realizing then that I could not tell her how she could have His answers. That didn't matter. She didn't ask. After simply looking at me, she then turned and walked off. Her hurt and anger, as I was to learn years later, did not go away.

Angry feelings never vanish by themselves, nor do they get better on their own. We search this book and that, attend workshops, join therapy groups. They help, but somehow the ache and the deep-down sense of something being wrong does not go away. Perhaps we read the Bible. "Let this mind be in you which was also in Christ Jesus" (Phil. 2:5, NKJV), we tell ourselves, and struggle even harder with our feelings. When change still does not happen, we seriously begin to doubt God's love.

Every age from long before Jonah's time to ours has experienced the same consuming anger. We, though, are even less capable in dealing with it. Flick through the television channels and you'll probably find at least six or seven programs acting out angry feelings. But almost nowhere, it seems, is anyone showing us how to resolve our anger. On our own, coping as best as we can, we grope our way through life. All the while, not even an arm's length away, God's healing is waiting for us. We don't have to go looking for it. Yet blinded by our anger and resentment, like Jonah, we struggle on, not seeing what God is trying to show us, not hearing what He is seeking to tell us, not knowing how to have the healing He offers.

JONAH AND NINEVEH

"Jonah went out of the city and sat down east of the city, and made a booth for himself there. He sat under it in the shade, waiting to see what would become of the city."

—Jonah 4:5

That's a good one. A prophecy come true. Wicked Nineveh was destroyed—as he'd said. Only not in the way he wanted. Imagine the change in that place. Must have been a shocker to the rest of the world. Nineveh repentant. Without its shrine prostitutes and cultic feasts. Jonah should have been proud. Imagine. A preacher converting an entire city! In only three days. Even the king. Wow!

And what does he do? Gets mad and stomps out and sulks and . . . And You put up with him?

Pardon? You're saying what about the girl and . . . ? But look what they did. She's hurting. You didn't do anything. How'd You expect me to feel?

You said what?

You are doing something?

Mercy?

Patience?

Forgiveness?

For even me?

But I don't know what You're talking about.

No! I don't want to talk about it. Not now. I need time to think.

CHAPTER 19

GOD SENT A PLANT

The sun blazed down, burning the earth, and the earth multiplied its heat. Jonah hunched under his rude shelter, appearing as nothing more than a misshapen, dust-covered hump. Streaks of grime, sticky and mud-colored, wobbled from both temples, giving his cheeks a strange, smear-tattoo marking. Below the edges of his head cloth miniature dust-covered bubbles pocked his forehead. He faced westward, but his eyes had become vacant and unseeing. "I knew it." His voice scratched dryly through his throat. "I knew this would happen."

Lifting a hand, he unconsciously rubbed its back across his forehead, smudging the sweat and dust into a thin, yellow-brown mask. Other than that, he did not move, did not stir from where he sat. Time crept by, slowly turning day to night and night back to day. Again the sun began another journey through the brazen sky, glaring down in unfettered intensity. Instead of sweltering in the heat of this new day, Jonah sensed that it was growing somewhat cooler, more comfortable. He glanced above him, and at first he could not comprehend the message his eyes were sending to his brain. "A vine?"

He lay back and studied the thick layer of broad, protective leaves covering his shelter, shielding him from the sun.

"Ahhhh! God has seen my misery. He has sent relief in my time of pain." For the first time in weeks Jonah drew a long and satisfied breath, and he remembered again the psalm of thanksgiving he had prayed while in the fish. "Surely salvation does come from the Lord." And he let his tired mind draw consolation from his new comfort.

First a fish, then a vine. The inconceivable, then the insignificant. That is how God has worked through the ages. And that is how He works even today. He meets us where we are. First He thundered from Mount Sinai to get the attention of the slaves He had just delivered from Egypt. Then when they were ready for a fuller revelation of His character, He asked Moses to speak to the rock. To speak, nothing more. God had a great object lesson in mind. But pushed to the limits of his patience, Moses bungled it. "Must *we* bring water from this rock for you?" he bellowed at the complaining crowd. And he slashed at the rock. Twice. With that fiery outburst, Moses failed God. He missed the opportunity of demonstrating God's ultimate character—he failed at showing His quiet, constant, merciful, unfailing, and ever-present love (see Num. 20:2-12). Centuries later when a terrified prophet Elijah fled from the wicked Queen Jezebel, God revealed His true might to him in a *still small voice* (1 Kings 19:1-18).

God continues to disclose His greatest power through the seemingly insignificant. With a quiet voice He shares His most important truths. In His perfect timing, the proverbial straw that broke the camel's back becomes the piercing arrow that finally touches understanding and prepares the way for true change. I vividly remember my first visit to the village of the straight avenues and wide boulevards.

"Hang on!" Bob's voice sounded above the engine's roar. "This could be rough!"

Pressing my head against the Cessna's side window, I saw a long blotch of bare earth against the parched savanna. The runway. My hands instinctively gripped the sides of the seat just as the wheels hit. The plane bounced. Then settled.

Bob, not Rob, was our pilot then, and it was not only my first flight in; it was the first time ever for a plane to land there. When we rolled to a stop, the chief stepped forward.

"Hear the people!" he said.

The crowd's noise was impossible to miss.

"Some have walked all night to be here."

Five years earlier when he had left a well-paid government position to take hereditary leadership of his people, unrelieved poverty had welcomed the chief. Epidemics of cholera swept in with the yearly rains. And measles. Tuberculosis and malaria. Parasites and malnourishment. The village had no facilities for treatment, and no medications. Fresh graves, hundreds of them, followed the paths of the diseases.

The chief organized the people, and they began hacking out an airstrip with machetes and hoes. "When it's finished, planes can bring medicines," he promised.

A year later the strip stretched flat and clear.

"We need a clinic, too," he told the people.

They baked bricks and raised the walls.

Four more years passed.

The airstrip lay empty.

The clinic stood only as bare brick walls.

And they still had—

No nurse.

No medicines.

No vaccines for the children.

And no plane had ever come—not even one—until the day we landed. Men, women, and children danced and sang. They waved branches and shouted. Their smiles were broad and welcoming. We smiled in return. And we saw the children's bloated tummies and running eyes. Their wasted bodies and open ulcers. Their twisted legs.

"The people are very happy that you have come!" The chief's exclamation was almost lost amid their cries of joy.

But we were there to open a school and agriculture project, not to start a health center. We selected children to be sponsored, organized the school program, then left and sent JeanLuc to take charge. With his encouragement, the people started making bricks for the school. Then they completed the health center. A nurse came. The village children were studying, their sicknesses being treated. For a while everyone was happy. Precisely how the trouble started, no one can say for sure, but accusations began to fly and tempers flared. Work stopped. Then came the night of the mob, when JeanLuc and his family fled.

"The people won't work anymore," the chief confided the day I arrived with Rob and the children mobbed me. His *becauses* differed from JeanLuc's. "Politics and democracy," he explained. "Politicians tell the people that with democracy they don't have to work for their chiefs anymore. They don't have to make bricks or dig foundations or carry rocks . . ."

As he talked of their obstinacy, I felt my pulse quicken. *These are the ones who had chased JeanLuc. Refusing—in the name of democracy—categorically refusing to do the share of work required of them by their development funders.* "Not even to build classrooms for their own children?"

"Not even for the classrooms." The chief looked tired. "Maybe you can talk to them," he said.

I, indeed, had plenty to say.

In earlier years I'd surely have thundered out at them with an angry Jonah message, hard-hitting and hot, full of references to the justice they deserved and that indeed would fall upon them in the form of funding being withdrawn if they refused to cooperate. But something had happened.

GOD

Pardon?
Would You say that again, please?
Let's see. Did I get it right?

You're saying that
You see past sackcloth
and ashes,
and beyond the words of a prophet?
You know what prompts offerings and sacrifices,
and the thoughts inside a looks-good churchgoer?
You know when gifts are meant to build the person's image
and when they're prompted by seeing a starving
        prisoner?
You're saying You know all that because
You see inside minds
and understand motives
and hear hurting voices calling out?
And that while You don't usually send them,
You do speak through
earthquakes,
fire, and famine;
disease and debility;
success and failure?
That You use whatever is available in the individual case?

That for Jonah You used a fish?
That You felt bad when he ran?
That You wanted him to learn to trust You?
That You didn't have many choices out where he was?

You're saying that no matter how You have to do it,
You are always calling, "Come to Me."

But that not many hear or recognize Your voice?
That they run, fainthearted and fearful,
thinking You're out to get them for their sins?
You're saying that all You ever want is for
them to come to You?
That more than anything You want that?
And they just don't understand?
That's sad.
Pardon?
You didn't catch what I said?
I said, "That's sad."

CHAPTER 20

A SIGN?

Jonah, comfortable in his new shade, regarded the mysterious plant. "Maybe . . ." He bit his lower lip and studied the rich green leaves. "Maybe this is a sign." Rolling onto his side, he propped his head up with one arm. "A sign that God will honor my word." He dared to be hopeful now. "And will bring justice . . ." His focus blurred and his eyes stared into some unseen distance beyond the horizon, toward the sea, remembering the storm, the heaving deck, and how he had braced himself and shouted for the sailors to throw him overboard.

"And God sent a fish!" Astonishment swept over him again. "A fish! Surely . . ." Drawing a deep breath, he exhaled very slowly. "Surely God does perform mighty wonders. He will not disgrace me." And he sank back, hopeful that he, Jonah, would for all time be revered as a prophet of God. And he licked his lips as if in anticipation of the terror about to strike the city, as if in expectation of seeing tortured bodies writhing in the streets.

At that very moment God was looking on his heart, and what He saw—well, it may have been like on a certain morning when I'd finished making our bed. The bed didn't look right. Waterbeds shouldn't sag. Not even in Africa. But I saw a definite sag. Sliding my hands between the bed's wooden frame and the mattress, I started to tug back the heavy water bag to see what might be causing the unusual effect. Just then a gritty substance crumbled and my fingers pushed against something spongy and wriggling.

I gasped.

And jumped back.

And shook my hands.

Clay-colored grit flew everywhere.

And I saw a white thing. Wormlike.

On my hand.

Usually I don't scream.

But it wiggled.

When I finally stopped jumping and making noises and shaking the thing off my hand, I . . .

Well, I was home alone. Such situations must be dealt with sensibly. I moved slowly toward the bed again from another angle and reached across and grasped the tip edge of the liner. Taking a deep breath, and not daring to let my fingers slide down and touch any part of the frame I could not see, I clenched my teeth and pulled. A section of mattress eased away from the frame.

I felt my eyes grow bigger.

Thin, crooked trails traced the side of the frame and led down into the mattress support. And tunnels. Long, gritty, clay-colored, pencil-sized tunnels. My skin turned goose bumpy and crawly. Hand-width sections of the tunnels gaped open, and in them lay pale bodies. Hundreds of them. Tiny and pulsing, almost like maggots with legs. And I had touched *them*. I felt my grip weaken. Termites! In *our bed!*

The mattress smacked down with a splintering crack.

The bed sagged even more.

I watched it drop yet lower and lower.

Toward the floor.

My mouth dropped open. But I did not say a word. No words could equal the impact of the situation. The bottom of our water bed had just given way.

The termites, unseen and silent, had gnawed away at our bed's support. Pushed down and hidden, anger also wreaks havoc inside the person. Have you ever noticed that the more you dwell on angry feelings, the worse they get? That's a fact of anger. The more you think or talk about who and what has made you angry, the angrier you become. Unlike grief that dissipates by being shared or talked about, anger worsens. It turns easily to hate. "Be angry and do not sin," the Bible says. "Do not let the sun go down on your wrath" (Eph. 4:26, NKJV). But that's a tough order for an angry person.

In its purest form, though, anger is a good and acceptable emotion alerting us to certain dangers or situations that need to be corrected. As such, it is separate from sin. Pushed down and not dealt with, though, it enters the danger zone, pulling along our thoughts, turning them inward to dwell on ourselves. Dwelling on self is being turned away from God. Being turned away from God is self-centeredness. Self-centeredness is sin.

Sin, as we all know, has come down to us through a long self-centered history. As the old illustration tells us, "I" is always in the middle of sIn. Back when Satan was Lucifer, his thoughts began to focus inward. His divisive self-centered tactics got him thrown out of heaven (see Eze. 28; Rev. 12; Job 1, 2; Luke 10:18). To bolster his ego, Satan then set out and succeeded in tricking Eve through his appeals to her self-centeredness. As a result, we all have become victims of self-centered natures that pull us into sin. The horribleness of sin, though, is not, as many suppose, that it makes God angry. What disturbs Him is what sin does to us.

Anger becomes a sin when we choose not to control it. I remember the day I was left standing on the road, staring after Rigid Shoulders. I had no idea that choice or self-centeredness had anything to do with my being angry at her. As far as I knew, I had never made any conscious choice to be angry at anyone. I did not even like getting angry. It was embarrassing to be seen "flying off the handle." But no matter how hard I tried to hold my angry outbursts in check, someone or something would eventually push the right button and off I'd go again. Me—a Christian who truly thought that I was having a growing experience with the Lord. Throwing a verbal tantrum! Disgusting!

Then one day while we were grinding along another long and monotonous African road in our old four-by-four, something happened. I'd just come through another ego-ripping episode, the details of which are unimportant now. Angry at myself, I tried to escape my feelings by huddling on the jump seat with a book. Suddenly two sentences grabbed my attention.

"The secret is simply this: that the Christian life must be lived in the will, not in the emotions. God regards the decisions and choices of a man's will as the decisions and choices of the man himself—no matter how contrary the emotions may be" (Catherine Marshall, *Beyond Ourselves* [New York: McGraw-Hill, 1961], p. 56).

"The will!" A warmth as real as anything I had ever experienced wrapped itself around me. "My will!" Understanding dawned. I needed to yield my will to God. And right then and there I did.

I had long heard about yielding the will. Before that moment, though, I had no clear notion of what that meant. Actually, I didn't even know what exactly my will was. The encounter on the jump seat changed my understanding. It turned my Christian life around, starting me on a friendship relationship with God. Studying the Bible and biblical resource materials became an exciting hobby. In the process I discovered that the will is the governing and central power of our person. It is the power of decision, the power of choice. Yielding the will to God involves giving over every part of our personhood to Him, including our wishes, wants, thoughts, emotions, hurts, feelings, talents, passions, problems—everything. Even our anger.

The exact opposite of being self-centered, it is letting go of self-centeredness. It means giving up what we want and choosing to do what God wants. We *give our hearts to Jesus* and *are born again*. It starts us on the process of daily *dying to self*.

Emotionally and in theory, all Christians want Jesus in their hearts. That's taken for granted. Intellectually and in practice, though, most of us find ourselves before an almost-impossible hurdle when it comes to giving up what *we* want. Yielding the will is not an easy, one-time-for-all change. Sin will continue to trap us, and we may even still get angry sometimes. But God is only a *choice* away. Once we have made the initial choice, choosing to do His will becomes easier as we grow in Him.

"Now what?" I exclaimed that morning as I stood, staring down at our collapsed waterbed. I knew what needed to be done, but I did not want to do it. I wanted to go back to my computer, to lose myself in my writing and to escape the crawling sensation caused by seeing all those squirming, pulsing, ugly, pale termites. I wanted . . .

Gritting my teeth, I set to work, resolutely stripping off the bedding. Then I got the insecticide, the broom, and the hose after calling my husband from the mission office. When we finally had the water siphoned out of the mattress and the splintered wood, grit, and dust cleared away, we saw the tiny tunnel through a crack in the cement floor. "You'll need to plug that," Michele, the carpenter, warned when he came to take measurements for making the replacement parts. "And treat all the wood with oil so you won't have the same problem again."

Angry feelings—and sin in general—need to be dealt with just as thoroughly. Yielding the will to God is the only way to have complete healing. Comfortable in his shaded shelter, accepting it as a sign of God's care, Jonah had no idea of the self-willed condition of his heart. Nor did he know that God intended the plant as a lesson to help him see himself for who he really was.

JONAH AND THE WILL

The will—that's it! That's what You've been trying
to say. That when Jonah realizes his willfulness and yields
his will—

Yes. Uh—of course. I realize that now. That the same
goes for me. But . . . but . . . Why didn't You say
something sooner?

Oh. You've been trying?

But . . . it's not like I wanted to be bad or anything. I
. . . I just . . .

Pardon me?

Oh? It's the same for Jonah? He doesn't understand?
He doesn't know that he doesn't know You? He can't see
beyond his own feelings? You're saying that even when
You call someone, he or she still has to choose?

CHAPTER 21

THE BEST GIFT EVER

I know I'll burn in hell for feeling like this, but . . ."

It was the girl from the long-ago school, the one whose mirror could never agree with the principal's eyes. With the years she had become more lovely and poised, and to most onlookers, she was a perfect picture of the successful woman. Now, as she sat at the table, slumped forward, eyes downcast, I had the impulse to gather her into my arms and smooth back her hair and tell her that everything would be all right.

"I still hate them—the school, the church, those . . ." The color drained from her face as she sought to verbalize the intensity of her feelings. "They make me so angry. Thinking they're so good, while they . . ." Pausing, she lifted her head, and the blue eyes that had been so alight when we'd met were now flat and lifeless. "They're so *mean!*"

The immensity of the hurt from the rejection she still felt held her voice to hardly more than a whisper. Despite her poise and charm, she was inwardly a small, frightened child who, on her own, feared she could never measure up, either to the expectations of others or those of God. In her mind she saw herself as simply not good enough for anyone, especially not God, and she knew she could never fend off His wrath.

"I understand," I said, remembering how the rejection I'd felt from my small classmates had extended into adulthood, making me fearful and defensive. "People mean well, but . . ." A tall, bony woman, dress draping in proper modesty around her angular frame, hair stapled with long, gray pins into a precise French roll, haunted my own memories. Imagination labeled her *Grandmere* (French for grandmother) with the name to be mouthed in two distinct words, accent on the second. "Grand Mare!" She had operated as self-appointed watchman on the walls of Zion and frequently beckoned to one younger church member or another.

"Come."

The order initiated a march down the church stairs, into the basement, and toward the furnace room. Everyone knew about Grandmere and the furnace room. "Only place you can speak in privacy around here!" And everyone knew about Grandmere's lectures. "You!" Severe headshake and bony finger accusing. "However can you expect to please the Lord?"

No, the girl across from me was not alone in her hurt, but I'd long since found peace regarding Grandmere and the others young and old who, whether from ignorance or intention, had added to my pain. I prayed silently, asking the Lord for the wisdom to point her toward the same joy and release I had found in Him.

"Even if I go to hell," she repeated, "I can't help how I feel."

"Of course you can't," I agreed.

We cannot turn emotions on and off at will. They simply are. Anger is. Understood and kept in its proper place, it alerts us to situations that should, and often can, be rectified without conflict. Unresolved and stashed away, anger becomes . . .

"I hate them."

"I understand," I said again. From long and painful experience, I did understand. Repressed, unresolved anger can easily turn to hate. Hate is a deadly sin—on that the Bible is clear (see 1 John 3:15).

"I am so angry."

That admission, though she did not realize it then, was the first

120

step toward finding a resolution to her problem. Nothing can be re-solved, not even between us and God, until we recognize and admit that we have a problem. The girl had the self-honesty to admit her anger. Many churchgoers, though, thinking anger is wrong, fear putting their true feelings into words.

Another friend and I were out for a morning walk. Her neigh-bor Larry, a mutual acquaintance, joined us. A slender, intense man, Larry was well-known for his burden to convert *lost souls*, to bring them to the *truth*. "We've got to work harder." His voice was determined, his face tense. "We need more of the Spirit."

My friend and I agreed with Larry. We can never have too much of God's Spirit.

"I don't understand," he said. "I give out magazines and books. I visit people. I pray. Next month I . . ." He described a literature distribution project he had in mind. "I work hard for the Lord, but people just don't seem interested." Although he easily matched our stride, he had the air of a person who had already walked too far, as if he was carrying a heavy weight that made going difficult. "We need to work harder, pray more for the Holy Spirit."

The road looped downhill, a growth of spruce shading one side, the barns of a small farm standing on the other. "I wonder," I said, "if God sometimes sends His Spirit and we don't know it."

"Yeah." Larry spoke as though not hearing. "We've gotta try harder to do what God wants, pray harder."

"Maybe we're trying so hard to please Him that we don't get what He's seeking to tell us."

"Yeah. That's why we gotta pray more. We need His Spirit."

"Maybe we first need to make room for His Spirit by yielding our wills to Him."

"The will!" Larry's voice suddenly pitched higher. "That's what I don't understand. That part about yielding the will. I read about it, but . . ."

The road had taken an uphill turn, and our strides shortened.

From experience, I knew what Larry meant. Many Christians face the same question. The will is the strongest and probably most misunderstood power we have. After searching for the right words, I finally said, "Paul tells us to get 'rid of all bitterness, rage, and anger' (Eph. 4:31, NIV), and to have the same attitude as Jesus had" (see Phil. 2:5).

I knew I was speaking uncomfortably close to what Larry carried in his heart. In addition to having gone through a difficult divorce, he had also unfairly lost his job. But had I asked "Are you angry?" he would have said no. From earlier discussions I knew he believed that anger is a sin. In a way, it seemed that by working for the Lord he was trying to prove that he was not angry. Therapists call that denial.

"Yielding the will to God is the starting point for the process of becoming like Jesus," I added.

We talked about the will being our power of choice. By the time we had looped around and come back to the drive leading to his place, Larry had become very thoughtful. He, a determined, hardworking Christian devoted to his church, and the girl who had become so bitter against the church because of the way she had been treated shared a similar problem. Neither understood that the intensity of their feelings had built a wall between them and God. Neither understood that their own unconscious choices played a big roll in causing them to feel the way they did. And neither understood the power of the will.

For me, recognizing my own self-centeredness and understanding the secret of yielding my will to God happened in the same instant. Until then I did not realize that I could not make myself love God. Once I made the intellectual choice of exchanging my will for God's will, my emotions gradually began to change. It was like being in a retraining process. Not everyone has the same experience. Some from early childhood maintain a close and growing relationship with Jesus. Others undergo dramatic ups and downs, as did Peter. Still others encounter a onetime turnaround like Paul. Many of the rest of us are more like Jonah, learning a little here and a little there, not knowing that we do not understand what God is asking of us.

"The best gift we can ever give ourselves is to give ourselves to God," I told Larry. "It is by giving that we become changed."

THE WILL

Wow! There on the jump seat! It was like . . . Well, I can't put it into good enough words, but it was like by yielding my will to You that everything was going to be all happy-ever-after. Like in the Jonah story we'd told Joann. Only a million times better. It was exciting, yet I knew I didn't have to make some big deal about it or announce anything to anybody. It was more like, well, I just had to relax and let myself be Your person, and then together we'd bit by bit sort through and clean up the messy parts in my life.

Afterward, well . . . life is just as real as it ever was. Sometimes I forget and find myself in a real pickle—as Jonah did. But then I remember. And I know You're here. And . . . well, it's so good to know that I can choose to turn back to You, and that we can pick up and go on together.

Ahhh! I wish everyone could know You like that.

Pardon me? You want me to share what I've learned. That . . . but . . . I'm not sure if . . . Oh. You say to remember that You are with me. But . . . all right. Sure. If that's what You want. It'd be a pleasure.

CHAPTER 22

ONE HUNDRED
TWENTY THOUSAND—AND ONE

Jonah's vine-covered haven wrapped him in a sense of peace, and he slept well that night, content at last that God had his best interests in mind. When he awoke he stretched, yawned, and reached his arms toward heaven. Today would be the day. *The day!* He intended to sit back in private comfort and enjoy the fruits of God's justice. With a great show of lifting his arms toward heaven, he stretched again. The sun was climbing rapidly, and he could already feel the air getting warmer.

Why is it getting warmer? he suddenly thought. He looked up. A clump of drooping leaves hung above his head. Reaching up, he touched one. "My plant!" Impulsively he grabbed his robe and dashed outside his little leafy bower, his hurrying feet kicking up clouds of dust-gray sand as he circled his shelter. Leaves, pale and limp, dangled in lifeless clusters, exposing the vine that hung, shrunken and contorted, like the twisted skeleton of some many-armed monster.

"God!"

He stared toward the heavens. The sun climbed relentlessly, burning down. A sudden gust of wind swirled past him. Dry, scorching, as only the wind from the east can be. He could not escape the heat. Could not escape . . .

"God!"

Throwing his hands over his head, he bowed toward the earth, pushing himself back into the now-useless shelter. Hunched down. Hot. Miserable. Faint. "Ohh-h-h-h!" he moaned. "I'd be better off dead!"

"What right do you have to be angry about the plant?"

That voice. Again. Clear and unmistakable.

"The plant?" Jonah's first impulse was to ask, "Who says I'm angry about the plant?" But before he had a chance to think through what he was really feeling, he heard himself blubbering as he had as a boy when he'd been beaten for something he hadn't done. "I have every right to be angry. Angry enough to die!"

"About the plant, is it?" God replied. The voice echoed into the distance, disappearing into momentary silence. Jonah looked up, confused. Then the voice came again. "This plant that grew up in one night and then disappeared the next. You didn't do anything for it; you didn't make it grow. And yet you feel sorry for it!"

The words knifed into Jonah's mind. "Think about it, Jonah," they seemed to be saying. "You are angry about a plant! A silly little plant!" The voice became clear again, distinct. "Then shouldn't I have pity on Nineveh, that great city? After all, it has more than 120,000 innocent people in it, as well as many animals."

With that, the voice disappeared.

And Jonah's story abruptly ends.

The Bible gives no follow-up, no report of what happened to Jonah after that. God had the last word.

By extending what we do know of the prophet, we can imagine him sitting alone, humiliated, helpless, frustrated, hurt, confused, disappointed, dejected, and discouraged, positive that his reputation as a prophet was ruined, muttering to himself, "I knew it! I knew it! I. I . . ."

The tiny, one-letter word, the absolute center of the prophet's private world, suddenly stands stripped between him and the pagan city. Understanding knifes through his mind. God's justice—God's loving mercy. One hundred twenty thousand condemned individuals have been touched and changed. Have been saved. No! Make that 120,000—and one!

God is still searching for His own. "Come," He says. "Bring Me your burden of self centeredness. Bring Me your hurt, your anxiety, your resentments, your anger. Bring Me all of your problems." In exchange He offers us His healing. Healing, though, is a process that takes time, a process that will reach into eternity. When you go to physicians, their diagnoses and prescriptions do not instantly cure you. Healing happens over time as you take your medicine, change your diet, exercise, or do whatever is needed in your particular case. Similarly, yielding our wills does not instantly transform us into perfect, God-centered individuals. But it initiates a retraining process. As author Tim Hansel says: "We are human becomings" (*The Hidden Adventure* [Carmel, N.Y. *Guidepost*, 1987]).

By continuing to choose God's way, we experience on-going change. Our awareness of God sharpens, and we are more apt to recognize the revelations of His will to us through the Bible, through appeals of the Holy Spirit to our hearts, and through His providential outworkings. He also works on our behalf through dedicated Christian professionals, who teach self-help skills and techniques for dealing with and managing anger, and through fellow Christians as they share insights from their own growing experience with the Lord.

Grace, a young Christian who only a short time earlier had chosen to give her life to God, came to see me, her face showing the strains of inward struggle. Her full lips were tight, her eyes dull, her cheeks hard. "I'm so angry," she said, telling of stories circulating about her. "I want them to hurt, to pay for all the lies that they've told about me. What can I do?" she asked.

"Forgive them."

"Forgive?" The word seemed to fasten itself to her lips. "But . . ." Her eyes mirrored shock. "But how? Whenever I think about what they've said . . ."

I said something about how the more we think about what someone's done to hurt us, the more we want to hurt them back. "But Jesus has the answer."

Her eyes met mine. She said nothing.

"He said, 'Come to me, all of you who are tired from carrying heavy loads' (see Matt. 11:28-30). Angry feelings are among the heaviest, most tiring loads we carry," I continued. "He'll help."

"But . . ." The hesitation in her voice indicated a tornness between the urge to fight back and a desire to find relief from what she was feeling.

We talked about Jesus' struggle in Gethsemane. Since His birth He had lived God's will, had successfully met Satan's temptations in the wilderness, and had risen above accusations of every kind during His ministry. But that Thursday night in the garden the intensity of His feelings almost overwhelmed Him. He knew He faced an excruciating execution the next day, during which the sins of all ages would separate Him from His Father. The thought was almost too much. He struggled in prayer, wishing for escape. Finally he was able to say, "Not My will, but Yours" (see Matt. 26:36-46; Mark 14:32-42; Luke 22:40-46).

"But . . .What they've done . . ." Grace's voice reflected her own struggle.

"The antidote for angry feelings is forgiveness," I insisted. "Until we learn to forgive, we'll never be rid of our angry feelings. Yet without letting go of angry feelings, we can never truly forgive. Unless we let go and forgive, we'll never be able to forget, and those angry feelings will keep growing, and . . ." I could tell that my theorizing looped around her in a puzzling circle. What I was trying to share needed to be laid out in almost textbook form.

"To understand the relationship between forgiveness and anger, we need to grasp the differences between feelings and decisions and processes," I said, going on to explain that in a general sense *feelings* are reactions that simply happen. We do not reason them out and decide to have them. They just happen. *Decisions* are consciously and voluntarily made. A decision is the intellectual act of making up one's mind about something. *Processes* are continuing developments that take time. "Anger is a feeling," I said. "Acting out angry feelings is a decision. Forgiveness is a decision. Forgetting is a process."

"But I didn't decide to be angry . . ." she started to say.

I smiled. "Of course you didn't decide to be angry," I agreed. "Angry feelings can happen so quickly that we have no idea we're making any kind of choice." And I told her about anger being a secondary reaction to a primary emotion, that of itself anger gives us information about a situation. "Anger is a feeling," I repeated. "The acting out of angry feelings, though, is always a decision. So is forgiveness. Angry feelings and forgiveness cannot exist together." I went on to share more of the information I had collected about anger and forgiveness.

"Most people react to their anger either by spouting off or by pushing their feelings down inside them—bottling them up, suppressing them. Either way, they've made a decision, whether they know it or not, not to deal with the problem. Some angry experts . . ." I paused, then corrected myself. "Some experts on anger suggest four general ways for controlling angry feelings. First, admit to yourself that you are angry. Second, figure out what you're angry about. Third, decide if you are angry about something realistic. You've done all that, haven't you?"

She nodded. "Yeah, but what should I do? I want them to know that what they are saying is untrue and to go to everyone and tell them the truth."

I smiled again. "That's the fourth step—to correct the situation by taking reasonable action. But . . ." I drew a deep breath. "Even if you confront the guilty ones, your angry feelings won't necessarily go away. You need to add a fifth step. That is to do it God's way by forgiving . . ."

"But I don't want them to get away with thinking that what they've done to me isn't really important. I want them to know what they've done, that they've hurt me terribly."

"Sometimes we confuse forgiveness and pardon," I suggested, explaining that forgiveness is the decision to give up resentment against or the desire to punish someone for something he or she has done or is perceived to have done. "You want those who started the false stories about you to understand the wrongness of what they have done, to do what they can about correcting the gossip?"

She nodded again.

"Well, that shouldn't be a problem," I continued, "because true forgiveness separates the person from the act. Forgiveness is directed at the person. It does not necessarily lift the consequences of the act. Forgiveness does away with the desire to hurt the one responsible, but it doesn't have to take away punishment. For example, your little brother disobeys. Your parents forgive him. They still love him, but they punish him because they consider it as necessary discipline for his best good. Pardon, on the other hand, lifts punishment, but it does not have to include forgiveness. Offering forgiveness opens the way for relationships to be restored."

"But what if they don't accept my forgiveness?"

I shrugged. "That becomes their problem then, doesn't it? The important thing for you is that you have forgiven them."

"Even if I do forgive them," Grace said, "I'm not sure I can forget what they've done."

"Well . . ." I chuckled. "The old saying, forgive and forget, doesn't work quite that easily, does it? All sorts of things can trigger memories of what happened, but with time and with the consistent decision to not let yourself dwell on what happened, the memories will gradually fade away."

"I know God says He won't forgive us unless we forgive others (see Matt. 6:15; 18:35; Mark 11:25), so . . ." Grace let her voice trail away. "I'll think about what you've said," she promised when she left. "But it isn't easy."

Forgiveness seldom comes easily. My writing once trapped me in one of those proverbial comedy-of-errors situations. Representatives from a major funding group visited our mission. "You're a writer," they said. "We need some stories to promote what your mission is doing."

I had two stories in process that I had intended for a magazine. Instead of keeping them for it, I pulled them from my computer and printed them out in manuscript form. "Now, don't forget where you got these," I said.

They promised to not forget.

Returning to their more-than-busy home office, they handed the stories to someone else. From there, the stories passed from department to department. When furlough time came, we visited the agency. An apologetic rep called me into his office. "I'm not sure what happened, but there's a book . . ."

When I saw the book, the heat began rising upward along my neck. The title and the lead stories had come from the material I had sent—my stories. The ones that I had sent in good faith. And without so much as a word of thank you, or consideration of copyright, or of moral obligations toward me, the publicity department had paid another writer to change and use them as her own. Certain apologies were offered. I accepted them and decided to go on from there. Time passed. We were at a conference with others from the group involved. Someone mentioned the book. Suddenly I felt the heat rising again and had the urge to let them know how I really felt. Mumbling some excuse, I left and began pacing the hall. I did not want to give in to my angry feelings. More particularly, I did not want anyone to see me lose control. "God, what do I do?"

Desperate for an answer, I went to my room and picked up my Bible. It fell open to the book of Philippians.

"It is right for me to feel this way about all of you," the passage said. The words zeroed in like a personal message.

"Right?" I asked myself. "To feel angry?" I could not believe what my eyes were reading. Paul was writing about his joy and appreciation for the Philippians, and here I was, my heart taking in the message as though God were directing it toward my anger. As though He were saying that it was all right for me to be angry.

I read on. "And this is my prayer."

Understanding began to dawn.

"That your love may abound more and more . . . That you may be able to discern what is best and may be pure and blameless" (Phil. 1:7-11, NIV).

Paul's prayer made a perfect model for me to copy. I started praying it for the ones involved—that they would see what was best, that they would be pure and blameless. And I prayed the same thing for myself. As I prayed, my anger began to subside.

At the time I had not yet grasped the difference between anger and the acting out of angry feelings. I knew the principle of separating the act from the person. But I did not yet understand the importance of separating within my own mind the act of offering forgiveness, from the act of being honest about how the wrongful action had affected me. Even when the person is forgiven, his or her hurtful actions may still need to be dealt with. I had to go back through steps 3 and 4 for controlling anger and decide if it was legitimate for me to take further measures. If so, I knew I would have to do it in the spirit of forgiveness. In the end I addressed a letter to the one in charge of the departments involved, stating my position as clearly and as kindly as possible and suggesting measures that could correct the matter. The process of writing the letter so eased what I had been feeling that whether or not they agreed with what I suggested was no longer important. I had taken reasonable action—forgiveness was a fact.

Dealing with any wrongful situation proceeds much more satisfactorily if done in a spirit of forgiveness than if handled in anger. That was what I had wanted Grace to understand. It is also part of the message I have found in the story of Jonah.

Surprising as it may seem, the spirit of forgiveness comes down to us as part of the sign of Jonah. "You'll only be given the sign of Jonah," Jesus said to the unbelieving Jews demanding proof of His divinity. Then before He died on the cross he cried out, "Father, forgive them, for they do not know what they do" (Luke 23:34, NKJV).

JONAH AND FORGIVENESS

Forgiveness? That's the part I'm not sure about.
Jonah's book talks about You changing Your mind. Of
course, that means You forgave the Ninevites. But Jonah?
Did he ever forgive them? Did he ever resolve his anger?
Did he ever find Your healing? His story stops . . .

Oh! You wanted the story to stop there. At the
climax, the crowning point. You say that You didn't want
a recital of what happened next to blind our thinking.
That You want us to decide what we would have done had
we been in his place. H'mmm . . .

You're saying that I need to think it through for
myself? To see how it applies to me? OK, sure, I'll do that.

CHAPTER 23

THE SIGN OF JONAH

I dashed out the door and into the near-freezing dankness that comes with spring thaw on the Canadian prairies.

"Joann!" I shrieked.

Unmindful of the ooze and muck splashing up around my feet, I rushed onto the muddy drive. My 2-year-old turned and, with serious blue eyes, regarded me. Jonah, her biggest and most exceedingly loved dolly, sprawled in front of her. I lunged forward.

"Joann!" Worry pushed the decibels higher. She was just getting over a terrible sore throat and cold. "What are you doing in that puddle?"

Before she could answer, I pulled her to her feet. Water drained from her pink but now very muddy jeans. I pushed her in the direction of the house. She had been told to stay inside. Then I grabbed up Jonah. The doll dangled from my extended arm, tricklets of water tracing milk chocolate squiggles over it's chubby cheeks. More of the off-color liquid drained from it's clothes.

"What were you doing?" I demanded.

Joann stopped, and turned.

"Well? What were you doing?"

She looked up with her large, still-serious, and now very worried blue eyes. "Baptizing Jonah."

Though concern for her state of health provoked a much more

stern reaction than I prefer to admit, her acting out of what she had seen at church sets the stage for this last chapter about Jonah.

Jesus promised his hearers the sign of Jonah. When He was taken from the cross, He stayed the biblical "three days and three nights" in the tomb just as Jonah had been three days and three nights in the fish (Matt. 12:40). The previous night in the garden He had thrown Himself down and had begged God to let Him escape the horror of His imminent execution, His fear of being totally separated from God. "Father, if possible, spare me," He pleaded. "Yet not My will, but Yours" (see Matt. 26:36-46; Mark 14:32-42; Luke 22:39-46). And the Romans nailed Him to the cross.

In her childish innocence, Joann had baptized her much-loved Jonah doll in a spring-thaw puddle. As practiced in the New Testament, baptism symbolizes the process of an individual's death to the old person of sin, burial with Christ, and resurrection to a new life with God (see Acts 2:38; Rom. 6:2-8; 1 Peter 3:21). Jesus honored Jonah by making his experience symbolic of the death experience He Himself had to pass through in order to ensure our salvation. When we experience the baptism of dying to self and rising in acceptance of the salvation—in acceptance of the spirit of forgiveness—that Jesus makes available, we too become included in the sign of Jonah. But does this extended sign of Jonah reach back to include the prophet himself?

The Bible gives no direct indication that Jonah actually did change. But if the view is correct that Jonah did indeed write the book bearing his name, then we can assume that he had become a new man in God. Otherwise, how could he share the story of his own cowardly running away? For what other reason would he describe his own disobedience and his childish anger? With that assumption in mind, let's picture the prophet at his writing table, shoulders rounded forward, head braced on his hand, eyes staring into the distance. A touch of silver now streaks his hair and edges his beard. His face has strength of feature, and yet it shows the softness marking one to whom life has given special insight and understanding.

"Tell what happened."

Jonah sighed and shifted. "Make them pay!" That's what he had wished for the Ninevites. Justice. Pain for pain. Death for death. As he sat there, he had no way of knowing that Nineveh's repentance and change would not last, nor that more than 100 years later a prophet named Nahum would again predict the decadent city's doom. In 612 B.C. the Babylonians and the Medes destroyed Nineveh, and its ruins still lie desolate some 200 miles north of Baghdad. But Jonah knew none of that. Instead, he was remembering the eternity he had endured in the fish, his decision to obey, and his disappointment. "How can I help them see that You are merciful and loving and patient? That there is healing in practicing Your forgiveness? How, God?"

His eyes lingered on an indefinable something in the distance and the fingers of his right hand played through his beard. His beard would make any Israelite justifiably proud. It was full and long and thick and . . .

"Put it on a scroll."

Jonah chuckled at how the command broke into his thoughts. "Put it on a scroll? My beard?" He chuckled again. "No. My pride. Ahhh . . ."

He had come a long way. No one could comprehend what had happened to him unless he himself had passed through a similar change. Facing up to self. Coming to grips with selfishness. Accepting his own inability to deal with his anger on his own. Experiencing transformation in attitude, in understanding, in reasons for obedience. Jonah nodded thoughtfully. The prophet had gone to Nineveh because he'd feared what God would do to him if he didn't. And now . . . he shook his head, amazed at the transformation in himself. Amazed at how the better one becomes acquainted with the real God who is gracious and just and merciful, the more one changes. Obeying the requests of such a God makes plain good sense.

"Make it a sign to point others toward Me."

His story could help alter the course of lives to come. "But . . . the fish? How can I write something so inconceivable, so impossible, and have it be accepted for the truth that it is?"

"Put it in simple words," God said. "Show them how it happened so that they will know that I sent the fish. Reveal it so they will know that I am God. So they will know that I am loving and merciful and kind and patient and forgiving."

"So they will know," Jonah repeated thoughtfully.

Experiences exceeding the realm of the normal are not easily put into words that others will accept. Neither do they easily bridge a distant God with the reality of now. When Joann was 5 and going to kindergarten, and little brother Jonny was still at home, their grandpa lived with us. Grandpa liked math, and he and Jonny spent long hours talking about numbers. "What's 16 times 16?" Grandpa asked again.

Jonny was leaning against the arm of his grandpa's favorite chair. "Two hundred fifty-six," he responded easily, his 3-year-old treble voice clear and sure.

"And 15 times 15?" The silvery head bent forward, waiting for the response.

"Two hundred twenty-five."

The two of them never seemed to tire of their games. Then when the neighbors visited, Grandpa would say, "He's 3 and he knows his numbers. Tell them, Jonny, what's 16 times 16?"

"Two hundred fifty-six."

"And fifteen times fifteen?"

"Oh, that's easy!" One neighbor smiled knowingly. "Those are showpieces. How about a real test? Jonny, what's 6 times 6?"

"Thirty-six."

"Well! Then 3 times 3?"

"Nine."

Too often we leave our God in the realm of the showpieces. We learn about the 16 times 16 miracles, such as the fish and Jonah, and say, "That's God." We declare His omnipotence, omniscience, and omnipresence, and expound His expiatory sacrosanctness, theorize on its metaphorical implications, and tremble at the probability of the retribution of His indignant wrath. But that is not the real test of knowing God.

Although the mystery of godliness is beyond human understanding, God has come down to meet us where we are. He wants us to know Him in terms that are as real and as everyday as 6 times 6 or 3 times 3. "Come to Me," He continues to invite. "Give Me your hurt and your anger, and I will give you healing. Learn to know Me as surely and as concretely as you know that 3 groups of 3 make nine."

"But how can I say it so they'll understand?"

"Jonah. I'm with you. Write."

God has also called me to write. At my computer today, wondering how to tie together the understandings God has given me about Jonah and anger, I keep thinking of the village of the wide boulevards and straight avenues. We flew there again last month. Almost three years had passed since I had gone in response to the call for someone to help solve the problems created by JeanLuc's forced departure. On that visit, parents and others had crowded the large outdoor meeting place on the afternoon I was to speak. Instead of condemning their angry behavior and threatening to close the project, as they deserved, I talked from the heart of my own experience. "Forgive the past," I urged. "Reach across to your neighbors. Work together, make bricks, build. Walk with God. You will be happier and healthier." I talked about the school, about learning improved agricultural methods, about better nutrition. "And your children . . ." I left hopeful that they might take my words to heart.

Last month, as the plane zoomed toward the airstrip, the people, as always, rushed out to greet us. Children, hundreds and hundreds of them, as dusty and tattered as all normal village youngsters, quickly filled the streets. As we made our way into the village, some skipped ahead. Most, though, hung back, crowding in as close as they dared to pace us along the way to our lodgings. "Look at them!" I exclaimed to Euphrasie, the colleague who had come with me this time.

She nodded. It was her first visit to the village.

Pausing, I snapped a few pictures of smiling, dust-smudged faces, then waved toward a group of laughing, robust youngsters. "They look so different. On our first visit . . ." I remembered the children who'd collected along our way then. Solemn-eyed, many with the brittle hair and bloated tummies caused by malnutrition, others with raw and oozing ulcers, running eyes, and matchstick arms and legs. I saw none of that now. "They've changed!" A sturdy tyke, perhaps 4 or 5, reached up to shake my hand. "They are so much healthier!"

"I believe you," Euphrasie said. "That's the second time you've said the same thing."

Later the children and their teachers proudly showed us their new school buildings, solidly bricked and roofed, and their large, well-kept gardens. Change had come. Healing was in process. We too can have change and healing. God calls us to come to Him with our hurt and our anger. He asks us to give Him our self-centered willfulness. In exchange for this easy yet most difficult of all decisions, He offers us His healing. It is ours to choose.

JONAH AND ME?

How did I get these ideas about Jonah? Well, for starters . . . It's a good story, with a strong plot, with an angry, hardheaded main character. Mad at God, he runs, meets the unbelievable, changes, yet keeps his headstrong ideas. Like a lot of us. But God works on hearts. After I met God as a friend and we started cleaning up some of the issues in my life, I studied the Bible and read commentaries and encyclopedias about Jonah, about his times, about God. Researched about anger. Imagined how I'd have felt in Jonah's place. Put it together and . . .

How do I feel now?

Changed.

Changing.

Realizing that I have a long way to go.

But that doesn't matter now. I know God is with me. And . . .

The more I learn about how God related to Jonah and others in the Bible, the more I realize how merciful and just and gracious and good He is. He offers His healing, but His love is so infinite that we are totally free to choose.

JONAH AND GOD

"Now the word of the Lord came unto Jonah son of Amittai, saying . . ."

—Jonah 1:1

The prophet drew a deep breath and bowed his head. "Yes, Lord," he said. "I understand." Then he straightened and reached for his pen. These are the words he wrote.

139

RESOURCES

If you are among the many who are searching for help toward personal healing, or if you are looking for suggestions of ways to enhance your walk with God, you may find just what you need in one or more of the following. Skills suggested in these resources will be extremely helpful in dealing with various wounds that life brings, including anger. The deep healing process we all need, though, comes from only one Source, and I believe the most effective way to access that is by spending a quiet, thoughtful time each day with the Bible and God.

—Corrine Vanderwerff

Audiocassette and videocassette series

1. Life Skills training seminars, by Ron and Nancy Rockey, Christian counseling psychologists and family health educators, offer help toward healing damaged relationships in a life-changing manner. *Getting Personal*, a 10-session seminar in five two-hour videos, will aid your understanding of how childhood wounds affect our relationships and give pointers on how to leave those wounds behind. *Hungry for Healing* is an 11-tape audio set. For information on how to obtain these or to attend a three-day Life Skills Seminar, contact Ruth Lam at Faith for Today, P.O. Box 320, Newbury Park, California 91319. Phone: (805) 373-7683.

2. *Understanding My Anger*, an audiocassette clinic by Paul Hegstrom, deals specifically with anger and offers insights from a Christian perspective and information that can lead toward finding healing. For further information, contact Life Skills International, P.O. Box 31227, Aurora, Colorado 80041-1227.

3. *Whole Brain Living Strategies*, *Minding Emotions*, and other videocassettes and audiocassettes by Arlene Taylor offer insights on how to understand yourself better and to become the person God intended you to be. The information can help you to "reparent" yourself as necessary and enhance all your relationships. Contact Realizations, Inc., P.O. Box 2554, Napa, California 94558-0255.

Phone: (707) 554-4981. Fax: (707) 648-1965.
E-mail: success@napanet.net

4. *God In All 66* is an inspiring audiocassette series in which Graham Maxwell goes through the Bible book by book with a group of friends while asking the question What does this say about God? The background information given, the personal insights offered, the process of putting the various stories and passages into the context of the entire Bible and using the Bible to understand the Bible, can start you on an exciting journey into discovering the riches of the Bible for yourself. You can order this and other audiocassette and videocassette series from Pine Knoll Publications, 1341 Pine Knoll, Redlands, California 92373-6545. Phone: (909) 792-0111.

5. *Spiritual Fitness: the Gospel for Emotional Stress*, a five-cassette workshop by Richard Nies taped in 1980, discusses various emotional problems while making important differentiations between feeling good and doing good for self-centered reasons and God's way of being good. Also available from Pine Knoll Publications, 1341 Pine Knoll, Redlands, California 92373-6545. Phone: (909) 792-0111.

Books

Hansel, Tim. *The Hidden Adventure*. Carmel, N.Y.: Guideposts, 1987.

Hurnard, Hannah. "A Brief Autobiography." In *Hinds' Feet on High Places*. Wheaton, Ill.: Tyndale House. Pp. 305-317.

Marshall, Catherine. *Beyond Our Selves*. New York: McGraw-Hill Book Co., 1961.

Raymond, Gillian. *Dear God, Can You Wink? A Parents' Guide to Prayer*. London: Scripture Union, 1995.

Taylor, Arlene. *Back to Basics: Timely Tips for Building Bona Fide Boundaries and Optimum Self-esteem*. Brushton, N.Y.: TEACH Services, Inc.

——, and Lorna Lawrence. *Thresholds to Thriving: A Power*

Pack of Practical Rx's. Napa, Calif.: Realizations, Inc. 1995.

White, Ellen G. *The Ministry of Healing*. Boise, Idaho: Pacific Press Pub. Assn., 1988.

———, *Steps to Christ*. Boise, Idaho: Pacific Press Pub. Assn.